informationsources | inlinguistics

a | *bibliographical handbook*

compiled and edited by

Frank Rice

and

Allene Guss

Center for Applied Linguistics 1965

Copyright © 1965
by the Center for Applied Linguistics
1755 Massachusetts Avenue, N.W., Washington, D.C. 20036

Library of Congress Catalog Card Number: 65-19794
Designed by Frank Rice and Allene Guss
Printed in the United States of America

informationsources | inlinguistics

Introduction

The present volume attempts to meet the need for a handbook describing existing sources of information in linguistics and certain related fields. It is intended principally for the student of linguistics at the upper undergraduate or graduate level. The established linguistic scholar can therefore scarcely expect to find here any great amount of unfamiliar material, though he may note with surprise or disapproval the inclusion or exclusion of particular titles.

COVERAGE

The handbook attempts to provide coverage of all the major traditional fields in linguistics (e.g. descriptive, historical, phonology, grammar, dialectology, semantics, applied linguistics); of most of the major theoretical approaches to linguistic analysis (e.g. Prague School, tagmemics, transformational analysis); and of the major fields of linguistics and related disciplines (e.g. linguistics and anthropology, linguistics and psychology, linguistics and mathematics). But in order to stay within the prescribed limits of length, the compilers decided to reduce drastically the coverage of languages and groups of languages. Only "language families" or "areal groupings" have been covered (e.g. Germanic but not English; Oceanic but not Samoan), and here only major journals have been included. Thus the student whose main interest is in a particular language or languages of a particular family or area will have to turn to other sources.

Again, in order to stay within the limitations placed upon the length of the handbook, the compilers have in practically all cases sacrificed depth of coverage for variety. Certain kinds of material have been deliberately excluded as a result of decisions taken at the early stages of the work. Excluded are articles that have appeared in journals or other serial publications except when such articles constitute important sources of bibliography or history; Festschriften, because of their enormous numbers; and monograph series published outside the United States. But every effort has been made to retain what appears to be indispensable material in each of the subject fields represented.

Keeping in mind the person for whom this handbook is mainly intended, the American student of linguistics, the compilers have given particular attention to materials published in English, though due consideration has been given to material in French, German, Russian, with some representation for other languages. Concern with the student also accounts for the presence of a number of textbooks, or books that are adaptable for classroom use.

ARRANGEMENT

The arrangement by subject has been used throughout, i.e. bibliographies, periodicals, surveys, and the like are listed with the individual subjects. Thus, a bibliography of phonetics is under *Phonetics and Phonemics* rather than "Bibliographies", and a journal dealing with anthropological linguistics is under *Anthropologica* *Linguistics* instead of "Periodicals."

Categories like "bibliographies" and "periodicals" are here called form divisions, and while the types of materials vary in the different subject fields and not all types are found for all subjects, the same form divisions recur in many of the subject divisions of this handbook. With some slight variations as have seemed advisable under each subject, the form divisions are listed in the following order: Bibliographies; Periodicals; Monographs; Congresses and Proceedings; Maps, Atlases, Handbooks; Histories and Surveys; Theory and Method.

In this bibliography, complete bibliographical information for an entry is presented only once. A number in square brackets following a title is a cross reference to the principal entry.

At the end of the volume there is an author index.

ACKNOWLEDGEMENTS

A preliminary version of this handbook was drafted by Valdis J. Zeps, now at the University of Wisconsin. Certain additions and emendations to that version were suggested by Miss Claire Asselin, working under the direction of Professor Eric P. Hamp of the University of Chicago. The present compilers developed a new scheme of organization of the handbook, with the result that portions of the earlier version were deleted and substantial amounts of new material added.

In the preparation of this volume the compilers have had the generous assistance of colleagues both at the Center for Applied Linguistics and elsewhere, who have willingly answered questions and made suggestions for its improvement. Particular thanks are due to Dr. Charles A. Ferguson, Director of the Center for Applied Linguistics, and to Dr. William W. Gage, research linguist on the Center staff and Acting Director of the Languages Program. Thanks are also due to Dr. Martin Joos of the University of Wisconsin, who was Visiting Director at the Center as the work was reaching its final stages. Finally, grateful acknowledgement is made to the National Science Foundation for its support of this handbook through a grant (NSF–18866) to the Center for Applied Linguistics.

F.R.
A.G.

Washington, D.C.

Table of Contents

INTRODUCTION iv

1.   Fields Within Linguistics   1

1.1.   GENERAL WORKS   1
Bibliography [001–011]
Periodicals [012–047]
Monographs [048–059]
Congresses and Proceedings [060]
Maps, Atlases, Handbooks [061–065]
Histories and Surveys [066–083]
Theory and Method [084–121]
General [084–111]
Descriptive [112–116]
Historical [117–121]

1.2.   TERMINOLOGY [122–128]   10

1.3.   PHONETICS AND PHONEMICS   11
Bibliography [129–130]
Periodicals [131–139]
Congresses and Proceedings [140]
Histories and Surveys [141–142]
Theory and Method [143–170]

1.4.   MORPHOLOGY AND SYNTAX   13
Bibliography [171–172]
Theory and Method [173–188]

1.5.   SEMANTICS [189–200]   14

1.6.   LEXICOGRAPHY AND LEXICOLOGY   15
Bibliography [201–205]
Periodicals [206–207]
Histories and Surveys [208]
Theory and Method [209–214]

1.7.   LINGUISTIC GEOGRAPHY AND DIALECTOLOGY   16
Bibliography [215]
Periodicals [216–220]
Theory and Method [221–233]

1.8.   SCRIPTS, WRITING SYSTEMS, ORTHOGRAPHIES   17
Bibliography [234]
Histories and Surveys; Theory and Method [235–249]

1.9.   LANGUAGE FAMILIES AND AREAS   18

African [250–255]
Caucasian [256]
Celtic [257–260]
Chinese [261–262]
Germanic [263–268]
Greek and Latin [269–273]
Indo-European [274–278]
Indo-Iranian [279]
Japanese [280]
Near Eastern and Oriental [281–290]
Oceanic [291–293]
Romance [294–301]
Slavic [302–314]
Uralic-Altaic [315–318]

2.   **Linguistics and Related Disciplines**   23

2.1.   GENERAL WORKS   23

Periodicals; Monographs [319–320]
Theory and Method [321–328]

2.2.   ANTHROPOLOGICAL LINGUISTICS   24

Bibliography [239–331]
Periodicals [332–337]
Monographs [338–339]
Histories and Surveys [340–342]
Theory and Method [343–345]

2.3.   SOCIOLINGUISTICS   25

Bibliography [346–348]
Periodicals [349–351]
Theory and Method [352–369]

2.4.   PSYCHOLINGUISTICS   27

Periodicals [370–374]
Monographs [375–377]
Histories and Surveys [378]
Theory and Method [379–393]

2.4.1.   CHILD LANGUAGE   28

Bibliography [394]
Theory and Method [395–402]

2.5.   MATHEMATICAL AND COMPUTATIONAL LINGUISTICS   29

Bibliography [403–411]
Periodicals [412–421]
Monographs [422–430]
Histories and Surveys [431–434]
Theory and Method [435–456]

3.   Applied Linguistics   33

3.1.   GENERAL WORKS   33
        Periodicals [457–462]
        Histories and Surveys [463]
        Theory and Method [464]

3.2.   LANGUAGE TEACHING   33
        Bibliography [465–470]
        Periodicals [471–476]
        Histories and Surveys [477–478]
        Theory and Method [479–492]

3.3.   TRANSLATION   35
        Bibliography [493]
        Periodicals [494–498]
        Theory and Method [499–504]

3.4.   STYLISTICS [505–513]   36

4.   Abstracts [514–527]   37

5.   Classification Systems [528–532]   38

6.   Manpower [533–537]   39

        AUTHOR INDEX   40

Part 1: Fields Within Linguistics

1.1. General Works

BIBLIOGRAPHY

001 "Annual bibliography for 19 —." *PMLA*. Publications of the Modern Language Association of America. New York, 1919 —.

   For the period 1919–1956, MLA published an annual "American Bibliography for 19 —" limited to American authors. Current bibliography, 1956 —, international in coverage. It appears in the May issue with the bibliography of the preceding year.

002 *Bibliografičeskij ukazatel' literatury po jazykoznaniju izdannoj v SSSR s 1918 po 1960 god* [Bibliographical guide of linguistic work published in the USSR from 1918 to 1960]. 2 vols. Moscow: Akad. Nauk SSSR, Inst. Jazykoznanija, 1958–63.

   Volume I covers the years 1918–55; Volume II, which is annotated, covers the period 1956–60.

003 *Bibliography of the Summer Institute of Linguistics*. Santa Ana, Calif.: Summer Institute of Linguistics, 1964. 64 pp.

   Mainly a listing of work done by SIL on some 200 tribal languages.

004 Comité International Permanent des Linguistes. *Bibliographie linguistique de l'année 19 — et complément des années précédentes*. Utrecht & Antwerp: Spectrum, 1949 —. Annual.

   International bibliography covering all fields of linguistics. Vols. I and II cover the period 1939–1947; separate volumes for each year thereafter. Entries in original languages with translation into French or English for some languages. Contains an index of authors.

005 *Dissertations in linguistics: 1957–63*. Washington, D.C.: Center for Applied Linguistics, 1964. 19 pp.

   Contains 268 entries. Each entry gives author's name, dissertation title, university which granted the degree, and year degree was granted.

006 Gage, William W. *Contrastive studies in linguistics: A bibliographical checklist*. 2nd ed. rev. and ed. by John H. Hammer. Washington, D.C.: Center for Applied Linguistics, 1965.

   Contains approximately 500 entries.

007 The English Association. *The year's work in English studies*. London: Oxford Univ. Press, 1919 —. Annual.

   Contains a section on linguistics. Includes comments on works listed.

008   Modern Humanities Research Association. *The year's work in modern language studies.* Cambridge: University Press, 1931 —. Annual.

Critical and selective. Limited to Germanic (excluding English), Romance, and Slavic.

009   *Quarterly check-list of linguistics.* An international index of current books, monographs, brochures and separates. Darien, Conn.: American Bibliographical Service, 1958 —. Quarterly.

010   U.S. Library of Congress. *East European accessions index.* Washington, D.C., 1951–61. Monthly.

A list of publications published in East Europe (excluding the Soviet Union), or the languages of the countries concerned, received by the Library of Congress and other American libraries. Contains subject index.

011   ———. *Monthly index of Russian accessions.* Washington, D.C., 1948 —. Monthly.

A list of publications in Russian issued in and outside the USSR that are currently received in the Library of Congress and a group of cooperating libraries. Contains lengthy subject index.

PERIODICALS

012   *Archivum Linguisticum.* A review of comparative philology and general linguistics. Glasgow, 1949 —. 2 nos. a yr.

013   *Acta Linguistica.* Revue internationale de linguistique structurale. Copenhagen, 1939 —. Irregular, 3 facsicles per vol. [Text in several languages.]

014   *Acta Linguistica Academiae Scientiarum Hungaricae.* Budapest, 1951 —. 4 fascicle per vol. [Text in English, French, German, or Russian.]

015   *Boletim de Filologia.* Lisbon: Centro de Estudios Filológicos, 1932 —. Quarterly.

016   *Boletín de Filología.* Santiago: Instituto de Filología, Universidad de Chile, 1937 —. Annual.

017   *Biuletyn Polskiego Towarzystwa Językoznawczego.* Bulletin de la Société Polonaise de Linguistique. Warsaw, 1927 —. Irregular. [Text in several languages.]

018   *Bulletin de la Société de Linguistique de Paris.* Paris, 1869 —. Quarterly.

019   *Cahiers de Linguistique Théoretique et Appliquée.* Bucharest: Acad. R.P.R., 1962 —. Irregular. [Text in several languages.]

020   *Cahiers Ferdinand de Saussure.* Revue de linguistique générale. Geneva: Société Genevoise de Linguistique. 1941 —. Annual.

021   *The Canadian Journal of Linguistics/ La Revue Canadienne de Linguistique.* [Formerly *The Journal of the Canadian Linguistic Association.*] Toronto, 1954 —. 2 nos. a yr.

022 *Cercetări de Lingvistică.* Bucharest: Acad. R.P.R., 1956 —. 2 nos. a yr.

023 *Foundations of Language.* International journal of language and philosophy. Dordrecht, Holland: D. Reidel, 1965 —. 4 nos. a yr.

024 *General Linguistics.* Lexington, Ky.: Dept. of Modern Foreign Languages, Univ. of Kentucky, 1955 —. 2 nos. a yr.

025 *Gengo Kenkyû.* Tokyo: Linguistic Society of Japan, 1939 —. Irregular. [Text in Japanese and English.]

026 *Indian Linguistics.* Journal of the Linguistic Society of India. Bombay, 1931 —. Irregular.

027 *International Journal of American Linguistics.* Baltimore & Bloomington, Ind.: Indiana Univ., 1917 —. Quarterly plus supplements.

028 *Journal of Linguistics* The Journal of the Linguistics Association of Great Britain. Cambridge, 1965 —. 2 nos. a yr.

029 *Kratylos.* Kritisches Berichts- und Rezensionsorgan für indogermanische und allgemeine Sprachwissenschaft. Wiesbaden, 1956 —. 2 nos. a·yr. [Text in English, French, German, and Italian.]

030 *Leuvense Bijdragen.* Tijdschrift voor moderne filologie. Louvain: Instituut voor Dialectologie, 1896 —. Quarterly.

Issues 1 and 3 contain the articles proper; issues 2 and 4 contain book reviews, bibliography, and a separate index. Text in several languages.

031 *Language.* Journal of the Linguistic Society of America. Baltimore, 1925 —. Quarterly plus supplements.

032 *Lingua.* International review of general linguistics. Revue internationale de linguistique générale. Amsterdam, 1947 —. 4 nos. a yr. [Text in English and French.]

033 *Linguistics.* An international review. The Hague: Mouton, 1963 —. Irregular. [Text in English, French, German.]

034 *Norsk Tidsskrift for Sprogvidenskap.* Oslo, 1928 —. Irregular. [Text in several languages.]

035 *Revue de Linguistique.* Bucharest: Acad. R.P.R., 1956 —. 2 nos. a yr. [Text in English, French, German, and Russian.]

036 *Ricerche Linguistiche.* Bolletino dell'Instituto di Glottologia dell'Università di Roma. Rome, 1950 —. 2 nos. a yr.

037 *Slovo a Slovesnost.* Časopis pro otázky teorie a kultury jazyka. Prague: Československá Akademie Věd, 1935 —. Quarterly.

038 *Die Sprache: Zeitschrift für Sprachwissenschaft.* Vienna: Wiener Sprachgesellschaft, 1949 —. Semiannual.

039 *Studia Linguistica*. Revue de linguistique générale et comparée. Lund, 1947 —. 2 or 3 nos. a yr. [Text in English, German, French, and Spanish.]

040 *Studies in Linguistics*. Buffalo, N.Y.: Dept. of Anthropology and Linguistics, Univ. of Buffalo, 1942/43 —. Irregular.

041 *Te Reo*. Proceedings of the Linguistic Society of New Zealand. Auckland, 1958 —. Annual.

042 *Transactions of the Philological Society*. Oxford, 1854 —. Annual.

043 *Travaux du Cercle Linguistique de Copenhague*. Copenhagen, 1944 —. Irregular.

044 *Travaux du Cercle Linguistique de Prague*. Prague, 1929–1939. [Ceased publication.]

045 *Travaux Linguistiques de Prague*. Prague: Académie Tchécoslovaque des Sciences, 1964 —. Biennial.

046 *Voprosy Jazykoznanija*. Moscow: Akad. Nauk SSSR, Institut Jazykoznanija, 1952 —. 6 nos. a yr. [Text in Russian; table of contents in Russian, French, and English.]

047 *Word*. Journal of the Linguistic Circle of New York. New York, 1945 —. 3 nos. a yr. plus supplements.

MONOGRAPHS

048 *Bobbs-Merrill Reprint Series in Language and Linguistics*. Indianapolis, Ind.: Bobbs-Merrill. [Facsimile reproductions of articles from scholarly journals.]

049 *Indiana University Publications in Anthropology and Linguistics*. Memoirs. (Supplement to *International Journal of American Linguistics*.) Baltimore & Bloomington, Ind.: Indiana Univ., 1948 —.

050 *Indiana University Research Center in Anthropology, Folklore, and Linguistics*. Publications. (Supplement to *International Journal of American Linguistics*.) Baltimore & Bloomington, Ind.: Indiana Univ., 1955 —.

051 *Language Dissertations*. (Supplement to *Language*.) Baltimore: Linguistic Society of America, 1927 —.

052 *Language Monographs*. (Supplement to *Language*.) Baltimore: Linguistic Society of America, 1925 —.

053 *Monograph Series*. (Supplement to *Word*.) New York: Linguistic Circle of New York, 1951 —.

054 *Monograph Series on Languages and Linguistics*. Washington, D.C.: Institute of Languages and Linguistics, Georgetown Univ., 1951 —.

055 *Papers on Formal Linguistics*. Edited by the Department of Linguistics of the University of Pennsylvania. The Hague: Mouton, 1962 —.

056 *Special Publications*. Baltimore: Linguistic Society of America, 1930 —.

057 *Special Publications*. New York: Linguistic Circle of New York, 1953 —.

058 *Studies in Linguistics: Occasional Papers*. (Supplement to *Studies in Linguistics*.) Buffalo, N.Y.: Department of Anthropology and Linguistics, Univ. of Buffalo, 1949 —.

059 *University of California Publications in Linguistics*. Berkeley & Los Angeles: Univ. of California Press, 1943 —.

CONGRESSES AND PROCEEDINGS

060 *Proceedings of the international congress of linguists*. 1930 —. [Titles and places of publication vary.]

MAPS, ATLASES, HANDBOOKS

061 Ichikawa, S., H. Kôzu and S. Hattori, eds. *Sekai gengo gaisetsu* [An introduction to the languages of the world]. 2 vols. Tokyo: Kenkyushu, 1952–1955.

062 *Languages of the World File*. A project under development at Indiana University. Compilation of essential data on some 3,000 languages. Reports on the contents of the File being published in fascicles in *Anthropological Linguistics*.

063 Meillet, Alphonse and Marcel Cohen. *Les langues du monde*. Rev. ed. Paris: Centre National de la Recherche Scientifique, 1952. 1294 pp. + maps.
The most comprehensive survey to date.

064 Milewski, Tadeusz. *Zarys językoznawstwa ogólnego* [Outline of general linguistics]. *Część I: Teoria językoznawstwa* [Part I: Linguistic theory]; *Część II:* [in 2 vols.] *Rozmieszczenie języków* [Part II: Distribution of languages]. Lublin & Kraków: Polskie Towarzystwo Ludoznawcze, 1947–48.
Part II, Vol. 1 contains the text of the survey, which is completely in Polish. Part II, Vol. 2 consists mainly of an indexed atlas of the languages of the world. Both maps and index are in Polish and English.

065 Muller, Siegfried H. *The world's living languages*. Basic facts of their structure, kinship, location, and number of speakers. New York: Frederick Ungar, 1964. 212 pp.
Covers 200 languages.

HISTORIES AND SURVEYS

066 Andrews, Schofield, Jr. and Joshua Whatmough. "Comparative and historical linguistics in America 1930–1960." *Trends I* [074], 58–81.

067 Arens, H. *Sprachwissenschaft*. Der Gang ihrer Entwicklung von der Antike bis zur Gegenwart. Freiburg: Karl Alber, 1955. 568 pp.

068 Battisti, Carlo. "Orientamenti generali della linguistica in Italia 1930–1960." *Trends I* [074], 240–82.

069 *L'école de Prague d'aujourd'hui. Travaux Linguistiques de Prague* 1. (1964).

070 Fries, Charles C. "The Bloomfield 'school'." *Trends I* [074], 196–224.

071 Godel, Robert. "L'école Saussurienne de Genève." *Trends I* [074], 294–99.

072 Hall, Robert A., Jr. "American linguistics, 1925–1950." *Archivum Linguisticum* 3.101–25 (1951), 4.1–16 (1952).

073 Hamp, Eric P. "General linguistics — the United States in the fifties." *Trends I* [074], 165–95.

074 Mohrmann, Christine, Alf Sommerfelt and Joshua Whatmough, eds. *Trends in European and American linguistics 1930–1960.* Utrecht & Antwerp: Spectrum, 1961. 299 pp. [Cited as *Trends I.*]

075 Mohrmann, Christine, F. Norman and Alf Sommerfelt, eds. *Trends in modern linguistics.* Utrecht & Antwerp: Spectrum, 1963. 118 pp. [Cited as *Trends II.*]

076 Pedersen, Holger. *Linguistic science in the nineteenth century.* Trans. by John W. Spargo. Cambridge, Mass.: Harvard Univ. Press, 1931. 360 pp. (Paperback edition: *The discovery of language: Linguistic science in the nineteenth century,* Midland MB–40.)

A classic study giving a detailed and scholarly account of linguistic history with special emphasis upon the development of Indo-European comparative linguistics.

077 Robins, R. H. *Ancient & mediæval grammatical theory in Europe with particular reference to modern linguistic doctrine.* London: Bell, 1951. 104 pp.

078 ———. "General linguistics in Great Britain 1930–1960." *Trends II* [075], 11–37.

079 Sebeok, Thomas A., ed. *Current trends in linguistics. 1: Soviet and East European linguistics.* The Hague: Mouton, 1963. 606 pp. [Cited as *Current Trends.*]

Contains studies of Soviet work on general linguistics, applied linguistics, and individual languages, language families and areal grouping, as well as surveys of the state of linguistics in other East European countries.

080 Sommerfelt, Alf. "The French school of linguistics." *Trends I* [074], 283–93.

081 Spang-Hanssen, Henning. "Glossematics." *Trends I* [074], 128–64.

082 Waterman, John T. *Perspectives in linguistics.* Chicago: Univ. of Chicago Press, 1963. 105 pp. (Paperback edition: Phoenix P–106.)

083 Zvegincev, V. A. *Istorija jazykoznanija XXIX i XX vekov v očerkax i izvlečenijax* [The history of linguistics of the XIXth and XXth centuries in essays and excerpts]. 2 vols. Moscow: Gosudarstvennoe Učebno-Pedagogičeskoe Izd., 1960.

Translations into Russian of selections from the writings of well-known philologists and linguists.

THEORY AND METHOD

GENERAL

084 Austerlitz, Robert, William Diver, André Martinet and Uriel Weinreich, eds. *Linguistic essays*. On the occasion of the Ninth International Congress of Linguists. (Publications of the Linguistic Circle of New York, 4.) New York, 1962. 219 pp.

085 Bazell, C. E. *Linguistic form*. Istanbul: ·Istanbul Press, 1953. 116 pp.
A critical survey of linguistic methods and theories.

086 Bloch, Bernard and George L. Trager. *Outline of linguistic analysis*. Baltimore: Linguistic Society of America, 1942. 82 pp.
Introduction to analytic methods in descriptive linguistics.

087 Bloomfield, Leonard. *Language*. New York: Holt, Rinehart & Winston, 1933. 564 pp.
A classic text in general linguistics. Bibliography most complete listing up to 1932. Extensive notes to chapters can also be used as classed bibliography.

088 Cohen, Marcel. *Le langage: Structure et évolution*. Paris: Editions Sociales, 1950. 144 pp.
An introduction to both historical and descriptive linguistic methods and results.

089 Firth, J. R. *Papers in linguistics 1934–1951*. London: Oxford Univ. Press, 1957. 233 pp.
A collection of essays on various aspects of linguistics.

090 Gray, Louis H. *Foundations of language*. New York: Macmillan, 1939. 530 pp.
Concentrates mainly on historical and comparative linguistics. Contains extensive classed annotated bibliography of the languages of the world and the history of linguistics, as well as a 70-page index.

091 Greenberg, Joseph H. *Essays in linguistics*. Chicago: Univ. of Chicago Press, 1957. 108 pp. (Paperback edition: Phoenix P–119.)
Essays dealing with methodology of language description, historical linguistics, and relationship between language and culture.

092 ———, ed. *Universals of language*. Cambridge, Mass.: M.I.T. Press, 1963. 269 pp.
Contains papers on phonology, grammar, semantics, synchronic and diachronic linguistics, as well as summaries on language universals from the viewpoints of linguistics, anthropology, and psychology. Extensive bibliography.

093 Hall, Robert A., Jr. *Introductory linguistics*. Philadelphia: Chilton, 1964. 508 pp.
Introductory text covering descriptive and historical linguistics, as well as linguistics and related disciplines.

094   Hjelmslev, Louis. *Omkring sprogteoriens grundlæggelse.* Copenhagen, 1943. 112 pp. Trans. Francis J. Whitfield, *Prolegomena to a theory of language.* Rev. English ed. Madison: Univ. of Wisconsin Press, 1961.

A statement of "glossematics". Deals with general criteria for language theory, specifics of language theory, and relationship of language to non-language.

095   —— and H. J. Uldall. *Outline of glossematics.* A study of the methodology of the humanities with special reference to linguistics. Copenhagen: Cercle Linguistique de Copenhague, 1957. 90 pp.

096   Hockett, Charles F. *A course in modern linguistics.* New York: Macmillan, 1958. 621 pp.

An introductory course covering descriptive and historical linguistics.

097   Jespersen, Otto. *Language: Its nature, development, and origin.* London: Allen & Unwin, 1922. 448 pp. (Paperback edition: Norton N–229.)

One of the most important older introductions to language.

098   Katz, Jerrold J. and Paul M. Postal. *An integrated theory of linguistic descriptions.* Cambridge, Mass.: M.I.T. Press, 1964. 178 pp.

Primarily concerned with abstract questions about the nature of language. Aims to provide an adequate means of incorporating the grammatical and semantic descriptions of a language into one integrated description.

099   Malmberg, Bertil. *Structural linguistics and human communication.* An introduction to the mechanism of language and the methodology of linguistics. New York: Academic Press, 1963. 210 pp.

100   Martinet, André. *Eléments de linguistique générale.* Paris: Armand Colin, 1960. 224 pp. Trans. Elisabeth Palmer, *Elements of general linguistics.* Chicago: Univ. of Chicago Press, 1964.

A general introduction to modern structural linguistics.

101   —— and Uriel Weinreich, eds. *Linguistics today.* (Publications of the Linguistic Circle of New York, 2.) New York, 1954. 280 pp.

Articles on various aspects of linguistics.

102   Meillet, Antoine. *Linguistique historique et linguistique générale.* 2 vols. Paris: Champion, 1921–38.

Classic study of the principles and methods of historical and descriptive linguistics.

103   Pike, Kenneth L. *Language in relation to a unified theory of the structure of human behavior.* 3 vols. Glendale, Calif.: Summer Institute of Linguistics, 1954–60.

Aims to relate linguistic behavior and non-linguistic behavior through an analytical approach similar to that already developed for structural linguistics.

104   Robins, R. H. *General linguistics: An introductory survey.* London: Longmans, 1964. 384 pp.

Primarily designed for specialist students of linguistics.

105   Sapir, Edward. *Language: An introduction to the study of speech.* New York: Harcourt, Brace & World, 1921. 258 pp. (Paperback edition: Harvest HB–7.)

A classic in the study of language phenomena.

106   Saussure, Ferdinand de. *Cours de linguistique générale.* Paris: Payot, 1916. 331 pp. Trans. Wade Baskin, *Course in general linguistics.* New York: Philosophical Library, 1959.

One of the most important texts on linguistics to be published in the twentieth century. Marks the beginning of scientific linguistics.

107   Sommerfelt, Alf. *Diachronic and synchronic aspects of language.* Selected articles. (Janua Linguarum, Series Maior, 7.) The Hague: Mouton, 1962. 421 pp.

Fifty-three articles covering a wide range of subjects.

108   Trager, George L. *The field of linguistics.* (Studies in Linguistics: Occasional Papers, 1.) Norman, Okla.: Battenberg, 1949. 8 pp.

An essay on the nature and aims of linguistic science.

109   Vachek, Josef, comp. *A Prague School reader in linguistics.* (Indiana University Studies in the History and Theory of Linguistics.) Bloomington, Ind., 1964. 485 pp.

A collection of papers on general linguistic issues by members of the "Prague School" linguistic group. Most of the papers come from the period 1928–1948.

110   Vendryès, Joseph. *Le langage: Introduction linguistique à l'histoire.* Paris: Albin Michel, 1923. 461 pp. Trans. Paul Radin, *Language: A linguistic introduction to history.* New York: Alfred A. Knopf, 1931.

A general introduction to language based on the theories of the French School. Contains good bibliography.

111   Whatmough, Joshua. *Language: A modern synthesis.* New York: St. Martin's Press, 1956. 270 pp. (Paperback edition: Mentor MD–209.)

Aims to bring together views about language developed in different fields of knowledge, such as communication theory, statistics, symbolic logic, acoustics, and neurology.

DESCRIPTIVE

112   Gleason, H. A., Jr. *An introduction to descriptive linguistics.* Rev. ed. New York: Holt, Rinehart & Winston, 1961. 503 pp.

An introductory textbook.

113   Harris, Zellig S. *Methods in structural linguistics.* Chicago: Univ. of Chicago Press, 1951. 384 pp. (Paperback edition: *Structural linguistics,* Phoenix P–52.)

Presents methods of research arranged in the form of successive procedures.

114   Hill, Archibald A. *An introduction to linguistic structures: From sound to sentence in English.* New York: Harcourt, Brace & World, 1958. 496 pp.

An introductory text in descriptive linguistics. Examples mainly based on English.

115 Joos, Martin, ed. *Readings in linguistics: The development of descriptive linguistics in America since 1925*. 3rd ed. New York: American Council of Learned Societies, 1963. 421 pp.

A collection of forty-three articles with comments by the editor.

116 Trager, George L. and Henry Lee Smith, Jr. *An outline of English structure*. [Rev. ed.] (Studies in Linguistics: Occasional Papers, 3.) Washington: American Council of Learned Societies, 1956. 92 pp.

Important analysis of phonology and morphology of English.

HISTORICAL

117 Hoenigswald, Henry M. *Language change and linguistic reconstruction*. Chicago: Univ. of Chicago Press, 1960. 168 pp. (Paperback edition: Phoenix P–178.)

Analyzes certain formal properties of language change and makes explicit some of the procedures which lead to the reconstruction of change and to the discovery of lost language structures.

118 Lehmann, Winfred P. *Historical linguistics: An introduction*. New York: Holt, Rinehart & Winston, 1962. 297 pp.

Covers general principles of historical linguistics, procedures of gathering and analyzing material, and description of the processes of linguistic change.

119 Meillet, Antoine. *La méthode comparative en linguistique historique*. Oslo: Nygaard, 1925. 116 pp.

An important introduction to the comparative method.

120 Paul, Hermann. *Prinzipien der Sprachgeschichte*. Halle: Max Niemeyer, 1880. 288 pp. Trans. H. A. Strong, *Principles of the history of language*. London: S. Sonnenschein, 1890.

Covers the theory and methods of comparative linguistics prior to the development of descriptive linguistics.

121 von Wartburg, Walther. *Einführung in Problematik und Methodik der Sprachwissenschaft*. 2nd ed., enl. and rev. in collaboration with Stephen Ullmann. Tübingen: Max Niemeyer, 1962. 248 pp.

An introduction to historical linguistics.

1.2. Terminology

122 Felice, Emilio de. *La terminologia linguistica di G. I. Ascoli e della sua scuola*. Utrecht & Antwerp: Spectrum, 1954. 36 pp.

123 Hamp, Eric P. *A glossary of American technical linguistic usage 1925–1950*. 2nd ed. Utrecht & Antwerp: Spectrum, 1963. 62 pp.

124 Knobloch, Johann, ed. *Sprachwissenschaftliches Wörterbuch*. Heidelberg: Carl Winter, 1961 —. [Appearing in fascicles.]

125 Marouzeau, J. *Lexique de la terminologie linguistique — français, allemand, anglais, italien*. 3rd ed. Paris: Geuthner, 1951. 265 pp.

126 ———. *Slovar' lingvističeskix terminov*. [*Russian, French, German, English, Italian*]. Tr. by N. D. Andrejev. Moscow: Izd. Inostr. Liter., 1960. 436 pp.

127 Pei, Mario and Frank Gaynor. *A dictionary of linguistics*. New York: Philosophical Library, 1954. 238 pp. (Paperback edition: World Library WL–63.)

128 Vachek, Joseph, with the collaboration of Josef Dubsky. *Dictionnaire de linguistique de l'Ecole de Prague*. Utrecht & Antwerp: Spectrum, 1960. 103 pp.

1.3. Phonetics and Phonemics

BIBLIOGRAPHY

129 "Bibliography: Phonetics." *American Speech* [216], 1925 —. [Appears in February and October issues.]

130 Sebeok, Thomas A. "Selected readings in general phonemics (1925–1964)." *Studies in Linguistics* 17.3–9 (1964).

PERIODICALS

131 *Fonetica și Dialectologie*. Bucharest: Acad. R.P.R., 1958 —. Irregular.

132 *Journal of the Acoustical Society of America*. New York, 1929 —. Monthly.

133 *Journal of Speech and Hearing Research*. Washington: American Speech and Hearing Association, 1958 —. 4 nos. a yr.

134 *Language and Speech*. See [372].

135 *Le Maître Phonétique*. Organe de l'Association Phonétique Internationale. London, 1889 —. 2 nos. a yr.

136 *Onsei Gakkai Kaihô*. Tokyo: The Phonetic Society of Japan, 1926 —. Quarterly. [Text in Japanese with English summaries.]

137 *Phonetica*. International journal of phonetics. Basel, 1957 —. Quarterly. [Text in English, French, and German.]

138 *Studia Phonologica*. Kyoto: Institution for Phonetic Sciences, University of Kyoto, 1961 —. Annual. [Text in Japanese, English and German.]

139 *Zeitschrift für Phonetik, Sprachwissenschaft und Kommunikationsforschung*. [Formerly *Zeitschrift für Phonetik und allgemeine Sprachwissenschaft*.] Berlin, 1947 —. 4 nos. a yr. [Text in English, French, German and Russian.]

CONGRESSES AND PROCEEDINGS

140 *Proceedings of the international congress of phonetic sciences*. 1932 —. [Titles and places of publication vary.]

HISTORIES AND SURVEYS

141 Albright, Robert William. *The international phonetic alphabet: Its background and development*. (Indiana University Research Center in Anthropology, Folklore, and Linguistics, Publication 7.) Bloomington, Ind., 1958. 78 pp.

142   Allen, W. S. *Phonetics in ancient India.* (London Oriental Series, 1.) London: Oxford Univ. Press, 1953. 96 pp.

THEORY AND METHOD

143   Grammont, M. *Traité de phonétique.* 6th ed. Paris: Delagrave, 1960. 480 pp.

144   Halle, Morris. *The sound pattern of Russian: A linguistic and acoustical investigation.* With an excursus on the contextual variants of the Russian vowels, by Lawrence G. Jones. The Hague: Mouton, 1959. 206 pp.

145   Heffner, Roe-Merrill S. *General phonetics.* Madison, Wisc.: Univ. of Wisconsin Press, 1950. 253 pp.

146   Hockett, Charles F. *A manual of phonology.* (Indiana University Publications in Anthropology and Linguistics, Memoir 11.) Bloomington, Ind., 1955, 246 pp.

147   International Phonetic Association. *The principles of the International Phonetics Association,* being a description of the International Phonetics Alphabet and the manner of using it. London, 1949. 53 pp.

148   Jakobson, Roman. *Selected writings. I: Phonological studies.* The Hague: Mouton, 1962. 688 pp.

149   ———— Gunnar Fant and Morris Halle. *Preliminaries to speech analysis.* The distinctive features and their correlates. Cambridge, Mass.: M.I.T. Acoustics Laboratory, 1952. 58 pp.

150   Jones, Daniel. *The phoneme: Its nature and use.* 2nd ed. Cambridge: Heffer, 1962. 267 pp.

151   Joos, Martin. *Acoustic phonetics.* (Language Monograph, 23.) Baltimore: Linguistic Society of America, 1948. 136 pp.

152   Kaiser, Louise, ed. *Manual of phonetics.* Amsterdam: North-Holland Pub., 1957. 460 pp.

153   Ladefoged, Peter. *Elements of acoustic phonetics.* Chicago: Univ. of Chicago Press, 1962. 118 pp.

154   Martinet, André. *La description phonologique avec application au parler franco-provençal d'Hauteville (Savoie).* Geneva: Droz, 1956. 108 pp.

155   ————. *Économie des changements phonétiques: Traité de phonologie diachronique.* Bern: A. Francke, 1955. 395 pp.

156   ————. *Phonology as functional phonetics.* (Publications of the Philological Society, 15.) London: Oxford Univ. Press, 1949. 40 pp.

157   Mol, H. *Fundamentals of phonetics: I. The organ of hearing.* (Janua Linguarum, Series Minor, 26.) The Hague: Mouton, 1963. 70 pp.

158   Pike, Kenneth L. *Phonemics.* A technique for reducing languages to writing. Ann Arbor, Mich.: Univ. of Michigan Press, 1947. 254 pp.

159   ————. *Phonetics.* A critical analysis of phonetic theory and a technique for the practical description of sounds. Ann Arbor, Mich.: Univ. of Michigan Press, 1943. 182 pp.

160   ———. *Tone languages.* Ann Arbor, Mich.: Univ. of Michigan Press, 1948. 187 pp.

161   Potter, Ralph K., George A. Kopp and Harriet C. Green. *Visible speech.* New York: Van Nostrand, 1947. 441 pp.

162   Pulgram, Ernst. *Introduction to the spectography of speech.* (Janua Linguarum, Series Minor, 7.) The Hague: Mouton, 1959. 174 pp.

163   Šaumjan, S. K. *Problemy teoretičeskoj fonologii* [Problems of theoretical phonology]. Moscow: Izd. Akad. Nauk SSSR, 1962. 194 pp.

164   Smalley, William A. *Manual of articulatory phonetics.* 2 vols. Tarrytown, N.Y.: Division of Foreign Missions, NCCC, 1961–62.

165   Stetson, Raymond H. *Motor phonetics.* A study of speech movements in action. Amsterdam: North-Holland Pub., 1951. 212 pp.

166   Trubetskoy, N. S. *Grundzüge der Phonologie.* Prague: Cercle Linguistique, 1939. 271 pp. Trans. J. Cantineau, *Principes de phonologie.* Paris: Klincksieck, 1949.

167   Twaddell, W. Freeman. *On defining the phoneme.* (Language Monograph, 16.) Baltimore: Linguistic Society of America, 1935. 62 pp.

168   von Essen, Otto. *Allgemeine und angewandte Phonetik.* 3rd ed. Berlin: Akademie Verlag, 1962. 228 pp.

169   Westermann, Diedrich and Ida C. Ward. *Practical phonetics for students of African languages.* London: Oxford Univ. Press, 1933. 227 pp.

170   Wise, C. M. *Applied phonetics.* Englewood Cliffs, N.J.: Prentice-Hall, 1957. 546 pp.

1.4. Morphology and Syntax

BIBLIOGRAPHY

171   Boyd, Julian C. and Harold V. King. "Annotated bibliography of generative grammar." *Language Learning* 12:4. 307–12 (1962).

172   Bursill-Hall, G. L. "Bibliography: Theories of syntactic analysis." *Studies in Linguistics* 16.100–12 (1962).

THEORY AND METHOD

173   Axmanova, O. S. and G. B. Mikaèljan. *Sovremennye sintaksičeskie teorii* [Current syntactic theories]. Moscow: Izd. Moskovskogo Univ., 1963.

174   Bach, Emmon. *An introduction to transformational grammars.* New York: Holt, Rinehart & Winston, 1964. 205 pp.

175   Chomsky, Noam. *Aspects of the theory of syntax.* Cambridge, Mass.: M.I.T. Press, 1965.

176   ———. *Syntactic structures.* The Hague: Mouton, 1957. 118 pp.

177 Elson, Benjamin and Velma B. Pickett. *An introduction to morphology and syntax*. Santa Ana, Calif.: Summer Institute of Linguistics, 1962. 167 pp.

178 Harris, Zellig. *String analysis of sentence structure*. (Papers on Formal Linguistics, 1.) The Hague: Mouton, 1962. 70 pp.

179 Hjelmslev, Louis. *Essais linguistiques. Travaux du Cercle Linguistique de Copenhague* 12.1–271 (1958).

180 Jespersen, Otto. *Analytic syntax*. Copenhagen: Munksgaard, 1937. 170 pp.

181 Joos, Martin. *The English verb: Form and meanings*. Madison & Milwaukee: Univ. of Wisconsin Press, 1964. 253 pp.

182 Juilland, Alphonse G. *Outline of a general theory of structural relations*. (Janua Linguarum, Series Minor, 15.) The Hague: Mouton, 1961. 58 pp.

183 Lamb, Sydney M. *Outline of stratificational grammar*. Berkeley, Calif.: Univ. of California, 1962. 64 pp.

184 Longacre, Robert E. *Grammar discovery procedures: A field manual*. (Janua Linguarum, Series Minor, 33). The Hague: Mouton, 1964. 162 pp.

185 Nida, Eugene A. *Outline of descriptive syntax*. Glendale, Calif.: Summer Institute of Linguistics, 1956. 166 pp.

186 ———. *Morphology: The descriptive analysis of words*. 2nd ed. Ann Arbor, Mich.: Univ. of Michigan Press, 1949. 342 pp.

187 Postal, Paul M. *Constituent structure: A study of contemporary models of syntactic description*. (Indiana Univ. Research Center in Anthropology, Folklore, and Linguistics, Publication 30.) Bloomington, Ind., 1964. 122 pp.

188 Tesnière, Lucien. *Eléments de syntaxe structural*. Paris: Klincksieck, 1959. 671 pp.

1.5. Semantics

189 Baldinger, K. *Die Semasiologie. Versuch eines Überblicks*. (Deutsche Akademie der Wissenschaften zu Berlin, Vorträge und Schriften, Heft 61.) Berlin, 1957. 40 pp.

190 Bréal, Michel. *Essai de sémantique: Science des significations*. 5th ed. Paris: Hachette, 1921. Trans. Mrs. Henry Cust, *Semantics: Studies in the science of meaning*. With an introduction by Joshua Whatmough. New York: Dover, 1964. 341 pp.

191 Eaton, Helen S. *Semantic frequency list for English, French, German, and Spanish*. A correlation of the first six thousand words in four single-language frequency lists. Chicago: Univ. of Chicago Press, 1940. 441 pp.

192 Guiraud, Pierre. *La sémantique*. Paris: Presses Univ. de France, 1955. 118 pp.

193 Kronasser, Heinz. *Handbuch der Semasiologie. Kurze Einführung in die Geschichte, Problematik und Terminologie der Bedeutungslehre*. Heidelberg: Carl Winter, 1952. 204 pp.

194 Robinson, R. *Definition*. London: Oxford Univ. Press, 1950. 203 pp.

195 Stern, Gustaf. *Meaning and change of meaning*. Bloomington, Ind.: Indiana Univ. Press, 1964. 456 pp.

196 Trier, Jost. *Der deutsche Wortschatz im Sinnbezirk des Verstandes*. Die Geschichte eines sprachlichen Feldes. Heidelberg: Carl Winter, 1931.

197 Ullmann, Stephen. *The principles of semantics*. 2nd ed. (with additional material). Glasgow: Jackson, 1959. 348 pp.

198 ———. *Semantics: An introduction to the science of meaning*. Oxford: Blackwell, 1962. 278 pp.

199 Ziff, Paul. *Semantic analysis*. Ithaca, N.Y.: Cornell Univ. Press, 1960. 255 pp.

200 Zvegincev, V. A. *Semasiologija*. Moscow: Izd. Moskovskogo Univ., 1957. 322 pp.

1.6. Lexicography and Lexicology

BIBLIOGRAPHY

201 "Bibliographie des lexicales." *Cahiers de Lexicologie* [206], 1959 —. [Appears in each issue.]

202 Collison, Robert L. *Dictionaries of foreign languages*. A bibliographical guide to the general and technical dictionaries of the chief foreign languages, with historical and explanatory notes and references. New York: Hafner, 1955. 210 pp.

203 UNESCO. *Bibliography of interlingual scientific and technical dictionaries*. 4th ed. Paris: UNESCO, 1961. 236 pp.

204 U.S. Library of Congress. *Foreign language-English dictionaries*. 2 vols. Washington, D.C., 1955.

205 Zaunmüller, Wolfram. *Bibliographisches Handbuch der Sprachwörterbücher*. Ein internationales Verzeichnis von 5600 Wörterbüchern der Jahre 1460–1958 für mehr als 500 Sprachen und Dialekte. A critical bibliography of language dictionaries. New York: Hafner, 1958. 496 columns.

PERIODICALS

206 *Cahiers de Lexicologie*. Paris: Didier, 1959 —. Annual.

207 *Leksikografičeskij sbornik*. Moscow: Akad. Nauk SSSR, Otdelenija Literatury i Jazyka, 1957 —. Annual.

HISTORIES AND SURVEYS

208 Weinreich, Uriel. "Lexicology." *Current Trends* [079], 60–93.

THEORY AND METHOD

209 Axmanova, O. S. *Očerki po obščej i russkoj leksikologii* [Sketch of general and Russian lexicology]. Moscow: Učpedgiz, 1957. 296 pp.

210 Casares, Julio. *Introducción a la lexicografía moderna.* (Revista de Filología Española, Anejo 52.) Madrid: Consejo Superior de Investigaciones Científicas, 1950. 354 pp.

211 Chapman, R. W. *Lexicography.* London: Oxford Univ. Press, 1948. 34 pp.

212 Hallig, Rudolf and Walther von Wartburg. *Begriffssystem als Grundlage für die Lexikographie. Versuch eines Ordnungsschemas.* (Abhandlungen der deutchen Akademie der Wissenschaften zu Berlin, Klasse für Sprachen, Literatur und Kunst, Heft 4.) Berlin: Akad.-Verlag, 1952. 140 pp.

213 Householder, Fred W. and Sol Saporta, eds. *Problems in lexicography.* (Indiana University Research Center in Anthropology, Folklore, and Linguistics, Publication 21.) Bloomington, Ind., 1962. 286 pp.

214 Matoré, G. *La méthode en lexicologie. Domaine français.* Paris: Didier, 1953. 127 pp.

1.7. Linguistic Geography and Dialectology

BIBLIOGRAPHY

215 Pop, Sever. *Bibliographie des questionnaires linguistiques.* (Comité International Permanent de Linguistes, Publications de la Commission d'Enquête Linguistique, 6.) Louvain, 1955. 169 pp.

PERIODICALS

216 *American Speech.* A quarterly of linguistic usage. New York: Columbia Univ. Press, 1925 —. Quarterly.

217 *Fonetica și Dialectologie.* See [131].

218 *Orbis.* Bulletin international de documentation linguistique. Louvain: Centre International de Dialectologie Générale, 1952 —. 2 nos. a yr. [Text in several languages.]

219 *Publications of the American Dialect Society.* University, Ala.: 1944 —. 2 nos. a yr. [Formerly *Dialect Notes*, 1896–1939.]

220 *Zeitschrift für Mundartforschung.* Wiesbaden: Franz Steiner, 1924 —. 4 nos. a yr.

THEORY AND METHOD

221 Bach, A. *Deutsche Mundartforschung: Ihre Wege, Ergebnisse und Aufgaben.* 2nd ed. Heidelberg: Carl Winter, 1950. 335 pp.

222 Bartoli, M. *Saggi di linguistica spaziale.* Turin: Rosenberg & Sellier, 1945. 306 pp.

223 Cassidy, Frederic G. *A method for collecting dialect.* (Publications of the American Dialect Society, 20.) Gainesville, Fla., 1953. 96 pp.

224 Cohen, Marcel. *Questionnaire A et B pour enquêtes-sondages linguistiques.* (Comité International Permanent des Linguistes, Publications de Commission d'Enquête Linguistique, 1.) Utrecht & Antwerp: Spectrum, 1950–51.

225 Coseriu, Eugenio. *La geografía lingüística.* (Instituto de Filología, Universidad de la República. Publicaciones del Departmento de Lingüística, 11.) Montevideo, 1956. 47 pp.

226 Dauzat, A. *La géographie linguistique.* Rev. ed. Paris: Flammarion, 1943. 226 pp.

227 Gilliéron, Jules and Edmond Edmont. *Atlas linguistique de la France.* Paris: Champion, 1902–12.

228 Gilliéron, Jules and Mario Roques. *Etudes de géographie linguistique.* Paris: Champion, 1912.

229 Jaberg, Karl. *Aspects géographiques du langage.* Paris: Droz, 1936.

230 ——— and Jakob Jud. *Sprach- und Sachatlas Italiens und der Südschweiz.* 8 vols. Zofingen: Ringier, 1928–40.

231 Kurath, Hans, with Marcus L. Hansen, Julia Bloch, and Bernard Bloch. *Handbook of the linguistic geography of New England.* Providence, R.I.: Brown Univ., 1939. 240 pp.

232 McIntosh, Angus. *An introduction to a survey of Scottish dialects.* Edinburgh: Thomas Nelson, 1952. 122 pp.

233 Pop, Sever. *La dialectologie: Aperçu historique et méthodes d'enquêtes linguistiques.* 2 vols. Louvain: l'Auteur, 1950.

1.8. Scripts, Writing Systems, Orthographies

BIBLIOGRAPHY

234 Sattler, Paul and Götz von Selle. *Bibliographie zur Geschichte der Schrift bis in das Jahr 1930.* (Archiv für Bibliographie, Beiheft 17.) Linz, 1935.

HISTORIES AND SURVEYS; THEORY AND METHOD

235 Aguirre, Manuel. *La escritura en el mundo.* Madrid: Reliex, 1961. 514 pp.

236 Cohen, Marcel. *L'écriture.* Paris: Éditions Sociales, 1953. 138 pp.

237 ———. *La grande invention de l'écriture et son évolution.* 3 vols. Paris: Klincksieck, 1958.

238 Degering, Hermann. *Die Schrift: Atlas der Schriftformen des Abendlandes vom Altertum bis zum Ausgang des 18. Jahrhunderts.* 3rd ed. Berlin: Wasmuth, 1952.

239 Diringer, David. *The alphabet, a key to the history of mankind.* 2nd ed. New York: Philosophical Library, 1951. 607 pp.

240 ———. *Writing: Its origin and early history.* New York: Praeger, 1962. 261 pp.

241 Février, James G. *Histoire de l'écriture.* 2nd ed. Paris: Payot, 1959. 611 pp.

242 Gelb, I. J. *A study of writing: The foundations of grammatology.* Chicago: Univ. of Chicago Press, 1952. 295 pp. (Paperback edition: Phoenix P–109.)

243 Giljarevskij, R. S. and V. S. Grivnin. *Opredelitel' jazykov mira po pis'mennostjam* [Guide to the writing systems of the world's languages]. 2nd ed. Moscow: Akad. Nauk SSSR, Institut Narodov Azii, 1961. 302 pp.

244 Higounet, Charles. *L'écriture.* Paris: Presses Univ. de France, 1959. 136 pp.

245 Istrin, V. A. *Razvitie pis'ma* [The development of writing]. Moscow: Izd. Akad. Nauk SSSR, 1961. 396 pp.

246 Jensen, Hans. *Die Schrift in Vergangenheit und Gegenwart.* 2nd ed. Berlin: Deutscher Verlag der Wissenschaften, 1958. 582 pp.

247 North, Eric M. *The book of a thousand tongues.* New York: American Bible Society, 1938. 386 pp.

248 Palmer, Harold E. *The principles of romanisation.* Tokyo: Maruzen, 1931. 157 pp.

249 Smalley, William A., ed. *Orthography studies: Articles on new writing systems.* (Helps for Translators, Vol. VI.) London: United Bible Societies, 1964. 173 pp.

1.9. Language Families and Areas

AFRICAN

250 *African Language Studies.* London: School of Oriental and African Studies, Univ. of London, 1960 —. Annual.

251 *African Studies.* Devoted to the study of African administration, cultures, and languages. Johannesburg: Witwatersrand Univ. Press, 1942 —. Quarterly. [Formerly *Bantu Studies* 1921–1941.]

252 *Afrika und Übersee: Sprachen, Kulturen.* Berlin: D. Reimer, 1910 —. 4 nos. a yr. [Text in English, French, and German.]

253 *Bulletin of the School of Oriental and African Studies.* See [284].

254 *Journal of African Languages.* London: Macmillan, 1962 —. Quarterly.

255 *Journal of West African Languages.* Cambridge: Cambridge Univ. Press & Institute of African Studies, Univ. of Ibadan, 1964 —. Semiannual.

CAUCASIAN

256 *Studia Caucasica.* The Hague: Mouton, 1963 —. Irregular.

CELTIC

257 *Celtica.* Dublin: Dublin Institute for Advanced Studies, 1946 —.

258 *Etudes Celtiques.* Paris: Les Belles Lettres. 1936 —. Annual. [Formerly *Revue Celtique*, 1870–1934].

259 *Lochlann.* A review of celtic studies. Oslo: Oslo Univ. Press, 1958 —.
Irregular.

260 *Zeitschrift für celtische Philologie.* Tübingen: Max Niemeyer, 1896 —. 2
nos. a yr.

CHINESE

261 *Chûgoku Gogaku.* Tokyo: Univ. of Tokyo, 1952 —. Monthly.

262 *Chung-Kuo Yu Wen.* Feking: Jen Min Chiao Yu Ch'u Pan She, 1952 —.
Monthly.

GERMANIC

263 *Beiträge zur Geschichte der deutschen Sprache und Literatur.* Halle (Salle):
Max Niemeyer, 1888 —. 3 nos. a yr.

264 *Beiträge zur Geschich e der deutschen Sprache und Literatur.* Tübingen:
Max Niemeyer, 1955 —. 3 nos. a yr. [Assumes volume numbering of journal
of the same name published in Halle (Salle).]

265 *Etudes Germaniques.* Revue trimestrielle de la Société des Etudes Germaniques. Paris, 1946 —. Quarterly.

266 *Germanic Review.* Devoted to studies dealing with the Germanic languages
and literatures. New York: Dept. of Germanic Languages, Columbia Univ.,
1926 —. Quarterly.

267 *Germanistik: Internationales Referatenblatt mit bibliographischen Hinweisen.*
Tübingen: Max Niemeyer, 1960 —. 4 nos. a yr.

268 *Journal of English and Germanic Philology.* Urbana, Ill.: Univ. of Illinois
Press, 1897 —. Quarterly.

GREEK AND LATIN

269 *Glotta.* Zeitschrift für griechische und lateinische Sprache. Göttingen: Van-
denhoeck & Ruprecht, 1909 —.

270 *Gnomon.* Kritische Zeitschrift für die gesamte klassische Alterturswissen-
schaft. Munich: C. H. Beck'sche, 1925 —. 8 nos. a yr. [Text in several
languages.]

271 *Hermes.* Zeitschrift für klassiche Philologie. Wiesbaden: Franz Steiner,
1866 —. 4 nos. a yr.

272 *Latomus.* Revue d'études latines. Brussels: Société d'Etudes Latines, 1937 —.
Quarterly. [Text in English, French, and Italian.]

273 *Minos.* Revista de filología egea. Salamanca: Seminario de Filología Clásica,
Univ. de Salamanca, 1951 —. Semiannual. [Text in several languages.]

INDO-EUROPEAN

274 *Indogermanische Forschungen.* Zeitschrift für Indogermanistik und allgemeine Sprachwissenschaft. Berlin, 1891 —. 3 nos. a yr.

275 *Indogermanisches Jahrbuch: Bibliographie des Jahres 19 —*. Berlin: de Gruyter, 1913 —. Annual.

276 *Münchener Studien zur Sprachwissenschaft*. Munich: Münchener Sprachwissenschaftliches Studienkreis, 1950 —. Irregular.

277 *Wörter und Sachen*. Heidelberg: Carl Winter, 1913–43. [Ceased publication.]

278 *Zeitschrift für vergleichende Sprachforschung auf dem Gebiete der indogermanischen Sprachen*. Göttingen, 1852 —. 2 nos. a yr.

INDO-IRANIAN

279 *Indo-Iranian Journal*. The Hague: Mouton, 1957 —. 4 nos. a yr. [Text in several languages.]

JAPANESE

280 *Kokugogaku*. Tokyo: Society for the Study of Japanese Language, 1948 —. Quarterly.

NEAR EASTERN AND ORIENTAL

281 *Acta Orientalia*. Copenhagen: Societates Orientales Danica, Norwegica, Svecica, 1922 —. Irregular.

282 *Archiv Orientální*. Prague: Československá Akademie Věd Orientální Ústav, 1929 —. Quarterly. [Text in English, French, German, and Russian.]

283 *Asiatische Studien/Etudes Asiatiques*. Zeitschrift der schweizerischen Gesellschaft für Asienkunde. Bern: A. Francke, 1947 —. Irregular. [Text in English, French, and German.]

284 *Bulletin of the School of Oriental and African Studies*. London: Univ. of London, 1917 —. 3 nos. a yr.

285 *Harvard Journal of Asiatic Studies*. Cambridge, Mass.: Harvard-Yenching Institute, 1936 —. Irregular.

286 *Journal Asiatique*. Paris: Société Asiatique, 1822 —. 4 nos. a yr.

287 *Journal of the American Oriental Society*. Baltimore: American Oriental Society, 1843 —. Quarterly plus supplements.

288 *Journal of Asian Studies*. Ann Arbor, Mich.: Association for Asian Studies, 1941 —. 5 nos. a yr.

289 *T'oung Pao*. Archives concernant l'histoire, les langues, la géographie, l'ethnographie et les arts de l'Asie orientale. Leiden: E. J. Brill, 1890 —. Irregular. [Text in several languages.]

290 *Zeitschrift der deutschen morgenländischen Gesellschaft*. Weisbaden: Franz Steiner, 1847 —. 2 nos. a yr.

OCEANIC

291 *Journal of the Polynesian Society*. Wellington, 1892 —. Quarterly

292 *Oceania.* Devoted to the study of the native peoples of Australia, New Guinea and the islands of the Pacific Ocean. Sydney: Univ. of Sydney, 1930 —. Quarterly.

293 *Oceanic Linguistics.* Carbondale, Ill.: Southern Illinois Univ., 1962 —. Semiannual.

ROMANCE

294 *Revue des Langues Romanes.* Montpellier: Société des Langues Romanes, 1870–1939. [Ceased publication.]

295 *Revue de Linguistique Romane.* Lyon & Paris: Société de Linguistique Romane, 1925 —. Semiannual. [Text in English, French, German, Italian, and Spanish.]

296 *Romance Philology.* Berkeley, Calif.: Univ. of California Press, 1947 —. Quarterly.

297 *Romania.* Recueil trimestriel consacré à l'étude des langues et des littératures romanes. Paris, 1872 —. Quarterly.

298 *Romanic Review.* New York: Dept. of Romance Languages, Columbia Univ., 1910 —. Quarterly.

299 *Romanische Forschungen.* Vierteljahrsschrift für romanische Sprachen und Literaturen. Frankfurt a. Main: Vittorio Klostermann, 1883 —. Quarterly.

300 *Vox Romanica.* Annales helvetici explorandis linguis romanicis destinati. Bern: Francke, 1936 —. 2 nos. a yr.

301 *Zeitschrift für romanische Philologie.* Tübingen: Max Niemeyer, 1877 —. Quarterly.

SLAVIC

302 *International Journal of Slavic Linguistics and Poetics.* The Hague: Mouton, 1959 —. Irregular.

303 *Revue des Etudes Slaves.* Paris: Institut d'Etudes Slaves, Univ. de Paris, 1921 —. Irregular.

304 *Rocznik Slawistyczny.* Kraków: G. Gebethneri, 1908 —.

305 *Scando-Slavica.* Copenhagen: Association of Scandinavian Slavicists, 1954—.

306 *Slavia.* Časopis pro slovanskou filologii. Prague: Česká Grafická Unie, 1922 —. Quarterly.

307 *The Slavic and East European Journal.* Bloomington, Ind.: American Association of Teachers of Slavic and East European Languages, 1945 —. Quarterly.

308 *Slovenská Reč.* Časopis pre výskum a kultúru slovenského jazyka. Bratislava, Czechoslovakia: Slovenska Akad. Vied, 1912 —. Bimonthly.

309 *Studia Slavica.* Budapest: Academiae Scientiarum Hungaricae, 1955 —. Semiannual. [Text in Slavic languages. Summaries in English, French, or German.]

310 *Slavic Word.* A Slavic supplement to *Word.* New York: Linguistic Circle of New York, 1952 —. Irregular.

311 *Voprosy Slavjanskogo Jazykoznanija.* Moscow: Akad. Nauk SSSR, 1954 —.

312 *Die Welt der Slaven.* Vierteljahrsschrift für Slavistik. Wiesbaden: Harrassowitz, 1956 —. Quarterly. [Text in English, French, and German.]

313 *Zeitschrift für slavische Philologie.* Leipzig: Market & Petters, 1925 —. 2 nos. a yr.

314 *Zeitschrift für Slawistik.* Berlin: Institut für Slawistik in der Deutschen Akademie der Wissenschaft zu Berlin, 1956 —. Quarterly.

URALIC-ALTAIC

315 *Central Asiatic Journal.* International periodical for the languages, literature, history, and archeology of Central Asia. The Hague: Mouton, 1955 —. 4 nos. a yr.

316 *Finnisch-ugrische Forschungen.* Zeitschrift für finnisch-ugrische Sprach- und Volkskunde. Helsinki: Suomalais-ugrilainen Seura, 1901 —.

317 *Suomalais-ugrilaisen Seuran Aikakauskirja/Journal de la Société Finno-ougrienne.* Helsinki, 1886 —. 4 nos. a yr.

318 *Ural-Altaische Jahrbücher.* Wiesbaden: Harrassowitz, 1952 —. Semiannual. [Formerly *Ungarische Jahrbücher,* 1921–1943.]

SEE ALSO [012–047].

Part 2: Linguistics and Related Disciplines

2.1. General Works

PERIODICALS; MONOGRAPHS

319 *Sprachforum.* Zeitschrift für angewandte Sprachwissenschaft zur überfachlichen Erörterung gemeinwichtiger Sprachfragen aller Lebensgebiete. Bonn: H. Bouvier, 1955 —. 4 nos. a yr.

320 *Bobbs-Merrill Reprint Series in the Social Sciences.* Indianapolis, Ind.: Bobbs-Merrill. [Facsimile reproductions of articles from scholarly journals.]

THEORY AND METHOD

321 Brown, Roger. *Words and things.* Glencoe, Ill.: Free Press, 1958. 398 pp.

322 Cherry, Colin. On *human communication: A review, a survey and a criticism.* Cambridge, Mass.: M.I.T. Press, 1957. 333 pp. (Paperback edition: Science Editions 087–S.)

323 Carroll, John B., ed. *Language, thought, and reality: Selected writings of Benjamin Lee Whorf.* Cambridge, Mass.: M.I.T. Press, 1956. 278 pp. (Paperback edition: MIT-5.)

324 Carroll, John B. *The study of language: A survey of linguistics and related disciplines in America.* Cambridge, Mass.: Harvard Univ. Press, 1953. 289 pp.

325 Henle, Paul, ed. *Language, thought, and culture.* Ann Arbor, Mich.: Univ. of Michigan Press, 1958. 273 pp. (Paperback edition: Ann Arbor Paperback.)

326 Mandlebaum, David G., ed. *Selected writings of Edward Sapir in language, culture and personality.* Berkeley, Calif.: Univ. of California Press, 1949. 617 pp. (Abridged paperback edition: *Culture, language, and personality.* California CAL–5.)

327 Sebeok, Thomas A., Alfred S. Hayes and Mary Catherine Bateson. *Approaches to semiotics: Cultural anthropology, education, linguistics, psychiatry, psychology.* Transactions of the Indiana University Conference on Paralinguistics and Kinesics. (Janua Linguarum, Series Maior, 15.) The Hague: Mouton, 1964. 294 pp.

328 Spier, Leslie, A. Irving Hallowell and Stanley S. Newman, eds. *Language, culture, and personality: Essays in memory of Edward Sapir.* Menasha, Wisc.: Sapir Memorial Publication Fund, 1941. 298 pp.

2.2. Anthropological Linguistics

BIBLIOGRAPHY

329   Goodell, R. J. "An ethnolinguistic bibliography with supporting material in linguistics and anthropology." *Anthropological Linguistics* 6:2.10–32 (1964).

330   Hymes, Dell H. "Bibliography: Field work in linguistics and anthropology." *Studies in Linguistics* 14.82–91 (1959).

331   Siegel, Bernard J., ed. *Biennial review of anthropology.* Stanford, Calif.: Stanford Univ. Press, 1959 —. [Contains a chapter on linguistics.]

PERIODICALS

332   *American Anthropologist.* Organ of the American Anthropological Association and Affiliated Societies. Menasha, Wisc. 1888 —. 6 nos. a yr. plus supplements.

333   *Anthropological Linguistics.* Bloomington, Ind.: Anthropology Dept., Indiana Univ., 1958 —. 9 nos. a yr.

334   *Anthropos.* Revue internationale d'ethnologie et de linguistique. Internationale Zeitschrift für Völker- und Sprachenkunde. Fribourg: Imprimerie St-Paul, 1906 —. 3 nos. a yr.

335   *Current Anthropology.* A world journal of the sciences of man. Chicago: Univ. of Chicago, 1960 —. 5 nos. a yr.

336   *Man.* A record of anthropological science. London: Royal Anthropological Institute of Great Britain and Ireland, 1901 —. Monthly.

337   *Southwestern Journal of Anthropology.* Albuquerque, N.M.: Univ. of New Mexico, 1945 —. Quarterly.

MONOGRAPHS

338   *Memoirs of the American Anthropological Association.* (Supplement to *American Anthropologist.*) Menasha, Wisc., 1888 —.

339   *Viking Fund Publications in Anthropology.* New York: Wenner-Gren Foundation for Anthropological Research, 1943 —.

HISTORIES AND SURVEYS

340   Hoijer, Harry. "Anthropological linguistics." *Trends I* [074], 110–27.

341   Hymes, Dell H. "Notes toward a history of linguistic anthropology." *Anthropological Linguistics* 5:1.59–103 (1963).

342   Olmsted, David L. *Ethnolinguistics so far.* (Studies in Linguistics: Occasional Papers, 2.) Norman, Okla.: Battenberg, 1950. 16 pp.

THEORY AND METHOD

343   Hoijer, Harry, ed. *Language in culture: Proceedings of a conference on the interrelations of language and other aspects of culture.* Chicago: Univ. of Chicago Press, 1954. 286 pp.

344   Hymes, Dell H. *Language in culture and society: A reader in linguistics and anthropology.* New York: Harper & Row, 1964. 1020 pp.

345   Levi-Strauss, Claude, Roman Jakobson, C. F. Voegelin and Thomas A. Sebeok. *Results of the conference of anthropologists and linguists.* (Indiana Univ. Publications in Anthropology and Linguistics, Memoir 8.) Bloomington, Ind., 1953. 67 pp.

2.3. Sociolinguistics

BIBLIOGRAPHY

346   Haugen, Einar. *Bilingualism in the Americas: A bibliography and research guide.* (Publication of the American Dialect Society, 26.) University, Ala.: Univ. of Alabama Press, 1956. 159 pp.

347   Pietrzyk, Alfred, Janet Duckett and Kathleen Lewis. *Selected titles in sociolinguistics.* An annotated preliminary bibliography of works on multilingualism, language standardization, and languages of wider communication. Washington, D.C.: Center for Applied Linguistics, 1964. 192 pp.

348   Savitz, L. *Bibliography of material in the sociology of language.* Philadelphia: Temple Univ., 1963. 59 pp.

PERIODICALS

349   *American Journal of Sociology.* Chicago: Univ. of Chicago Press, 1895 —. 6 nos. a yr.

350   *American Sociological Review.* New York: American Sociological Society, 1936 —. Bimonthly.

351   *Cahiers Internationaux de Sociologie.* Paris: Presses Univ. de France, 1946 —. Semiannual.

THEORY AND METHOD

352   American Council of Learned Societies. *Conference on non-English speech in the United States.* (ACLS Bulletin, 34.) Washington, D.C., 1942. 89 pp.

353   Bally, Charles. *Le langage et la vie.* 3rd ed. Geneva: Droz, 1952. 165 pp.

354   Bram, Joseph. *Language and society.* New York: Doubleday, 1955. 66 pp. (Paperback edition: Random House SS–8.)

355   Cohen, Marcel. *Pour une sociologie du langage*. Paris: Albin Michel, 1956.
      396 pp.

356   Duncan, Hugh Dalziel. *Communication and social order*. New York: Bed-
      minster, 1962. 475 pp.

357   Ferguson, Charles A. and John J. Gumperz, eds. *Linguistic diversity in South
      Asia: Studies in regional, social and functional variation*. (Indiana Univ.
      Research Center in Anthropology, Folklore, and Linguistics, Publication 13.)
      Bloomington, Ind., 1960. 118 pp.

358   Guxman, M. M. *Voprosy formirovanija i razvitija nacional'nyx jazykov*
      [Problems in the formation and development of national languages]. Mos-
      cow: Izd. Akad. Nauk SSSR, 1960. 308 pp.

359   Jespersen, Otto. *Mankind, nation and individual from a linguistic point of
      view*. London: Allen & Unwin, 1946. 198 pp. (Paperback edition: Midland
      MB–46.)

360   Krejči, Karel. *Jazyk ve vývoji společnosti: Studie ze sociologie spissovného
      jazyka* [Language in social evolution: Studies in the sociology of the literary
      language]. Prague: Podroužek, 1947. 102 pp.

361   Lewis, M. M. *Language in society: The linguistic revolution and social
      change*. New York: Social Science Pub., 1948. 248 pp.

362   Vildomec, Veroboj. *Multilingualism*. Leyden: Sythoff, 1963. 262 pp.

363   *Multilingualism and socio-cultural organization*. A symposium presented at
      the 1961 meetings of the American Anthropological Association. *Anthropo-
      logical Linguistics* 4:1.1–64 (1962).

364   Ray, Punya Sloka. *Language standardization*. (Janua Linguarum, Series
      Minor, 29.) The Hague: Mouton, 1963. 159 pp.

365   Rice, Frank A., ed. *Study of the role of second languages in Asia, Africa,
      and Latin America*. Washington, D.C.: Center for Applied Linguistics, 1962.
      123 pp.

366   Segerstedt, Torgny T. *Die Macht des Wortes: Eine Sprachsoziologie*. Zürich:
      Pas-Verlag, 1947. 174 pp.

367   Sommerfelt, Alf. *La langage et la société*. Oslo: Aschehoug, 1938. 233 pp.

368   *Urbanization and standard languages*. A symposium presented at the 1958
      meetings of the American Anthropological Association. *Anthropological
      Linguistics* 1:3.1–41 (1959).

369   Weinreich, Uriel. *Languages in contact: Findings and problems*. (Publica-
      tions of the Linguistic Circle of New York, 1.) New York, 1953. 148 pp.
      (Reprinted by Mouton, The Hague, 1963.)

2.4. Psycholinguistics

PERIODICALS

370   *Contemporary Psychology.* A journal of reviews. Washington, D.C.: American Psychological Association, 1956 —. Monthly.

371   *Journal of Verbal Learning and Verbal Behavior.* New York: Academic Press, 1962 —. Bimonthly.

372   *Language and Speech* Teddington, Middlesex, Eng.: Robert Draper, 1958 —. Quarterly.

373   *Psychological Review.* Washington, D.C.: American Psychological Association, 1894 —. Bimonthly.

374   *Quarterly Journal of Speech.* Columbia, Mo.: Speech Association of America, 1915 —. 4 nos. a yr.

MONOGRAPHS

375   *Experimental Analysis of the Control of Speech Production and Perception.* Ann Arbor, Mich.: Dept. of Psychology, Behavioral Analysis Laboratory, 1961 —. Irregular.

376   *Speech Monographs.* Columbia, Mo.: Speech Association of America, 1934 —. 4 nos. a yr.

377   *University of Washington Studies in Linguistics and Language Learning.* Seattle: Univ. of Washington, 1964. Irregular.

HISTORIES AND SURVEYS

378   Proncko, N. H. "Language and psycholinguistics: A review." *Psychological Bulletin* 43.189–239 (1946).

THEORY AND METHOD

379   Axmanova, O. S. *O psixolingvistike.* Moscow: Izd. Moskovskogo Univ., 1957. 64 pp.

380   Bühler, Karl. *Sprachtheorie: Die Darstellungsfunktion der Sprache.* Jena: G. Fischer, 1934 434 pp.

381   Carroll, John B. *Language and thought.* Englewood Cliffs, N.J.: Prentice-Hall, 1964. 118 pp.

382   Cofer, Charles N., ed., with the assistance of Barbara S. Musgrave. *Verbal learning and verbal behavior.* New York: McGraw-Hill, 1961. 241 pp.

383   Cofer, Charles N. and Barbara S. Musgrave, eds. *Verbal behavior and learning: Problems and processes.* New York: McGraw-Hill, 1963. 397 pp.

384   Joos, Martin. *The five clocks.* (Indiana University Center in Anthropology, Folklore, and Linguistics, Publication 22.) Bloomington, Ind., 1962. 62 pp.

385   Miller, George A. *Language and communication.* New York: McGraw-Hill, 1951. 298 pp. (Paperback edition: McGraw-Hill 42001.)

386   Osgood, Charles E. and Thomas A. Sebeok, eds. *Psycholinguistics: A survey of theory and research problems.* With *A survey of psycholinguistic research 1954–64,* by A. Richard Diebold, Jr. 2nd ed. (Indiana University Studies in the History and Theory of Linguistics.) Bloomington, Ind.: Indiana Univ. Press, 1965. 300 pp.

387   Osgood, Charles E., George J. Suci and Percy H. Tannenbaum. *The measurement of meaning.* Urbana, Ill.: Univ. of Illinois Press, 1957. 342 pp.

388   Piaget, Jean. *Le langage et la pensée chez l'enfant.* Neuchâtel & Paris: Delachaux & Niestlé, 1924. Trans. Marjorie Gabain, *The language and thought of the child.* 3rd ed. New York: Humanities Press, 1959. 288 pp. (Paperback edition: Meridian M–10.)

389   *Problèmes de psycho-linguistique.* Symposium de l'Assn. de Psychol. Scient. de langue française. Paris: Presses Univ. de France, 1963.

390   Saporta, Sol, ed., with the assistance of Jarvis R. Bastian. *Psycholinguistics: A book of readings.* New York: Holt, Rinehart & Winston, 1961. 551 pp.

391   Skinner, B. F. *Verbal behavior.* New York: Appleton-Century-Crofts, 1957. 478 pp.

392   Titone, Renzo. *La psicolinguistica oggi.* Zürich: Pas-Verlag, 1964. 313 pp.

393   Vygotsky, L. S. *Thought and language.* Ed. and trans. by Eugenia Hanfmann and Gertrude Vakar. Cambridge, Mass.: M.I.T. Press, 1962. 168 pp. (Paperback edition: MIT–29.)

2.4.1. Child Language

BIBLIOGRAPHY

394   Leopold, Werner F. *Bibliography of child language.* Evanston, Ill.: Northwestern Univ. Press, 1952. 115 pp.

THEORY AND METHOD

395   Cohen, Marcel, and others. *Etudes sur le langage de l'enfant.* Paris: Editions du Scarabée, 1962. 194 pp.

396   Grégoire, Antoine. *L'apprentissage du langage.* 2 vols. Paris: Droz, 1937–47.

397   Gvozdev, A. N. *Voprosy izučenija deckoj reči* [Problems in the study of child speech]. Moscow: Acad. Ped. Sci., 1961.

398   Jakobson, Roman. *Kindersprache, Aphasie und allgemeine Lautgesetze.* Uppsala: Almqvist & Wiksell, 1941. 83 pp.

399   Kahane, Henry, Renée Kahane and Sol Saporta. *Development of verbal categories in child language.* (Indiana Univ. Research Center in Anthropology, Folklore, and Linguistics, Publication 9.) Bloomington, Ind., 1958. 65 pp.

400   Leopold, Werner F. *Speech development of a bilingual child: A linguist's record.* 4 vols. Evanston, Ill.: Northwestern Univ. Press, 1939–49.

401   Lewis, M. M. *Infant speech: A study of the beginnings of language.* 2nd rev. ed. New York: Humanities Press, 1951. 383 pp.

402   Weir, Ruth Hirsch. *Language in the crib.* (Janua Linguarum, Series Minor, 14.) The Hague: Mouton, 1963. 216 pp.

2.5. Mathematical and Computational Linguistics

BIBLIOGRAPHY

403   Balz, Charles F. and Richard H. Stanwood. *Literature on information retrieval and machine translation.* Oswego, N.Y.: International Business Machines, 1962. 117 pp.

404   Delavenay, E. and K. Delavenay. *Bibliography of machine translation.* (Janua Linguarum, Series Minor, 11.) The Hague: Mouton, 1960. 69 pp.

405   Gipper, Helmut and Hans Schwarz. *Bibliographisches Handbuch zur Sprachinhaltsforschung.* Cologne: Westdeutscher Verlag, 1962. 384 pp.

406   Guiraud, Pierre. *Bibliographie critique de la statistique linguistique.* (Comité international permanent des linguistes. Publications de Comité de la statistique linguistique, 2.) Utrecht & Antwerp: Spectrum, 1954. 124 pp.

407   Hays, David G. *Annotated bibliography of RAND publications in computational linguistics.* Santa Monica, Calif.: RAND Corp., 1964. 35 pp.

408   ————. *Bibliography of computational linguistics.* Santa Monica, Calif.: RAND Corp., 1965.

409   "Recent publications on computational linguistics." *The Finite String* [414], 1964 —. [Appears in each issue.]

410   *Soviet bibliography of foreign works on machine translation.* (Foreign Developments in Machine Translation and Information Processing, No. 122.) Washington, D.C.: Joint Publications Research Service, Dept. of Commerce, 1963. 126 pp. [Annotated.]

411   Walkowicz, Josephine L. *A bibliography of foreign developments in machine translation and information processing.* Washington, D.C.: National Bureau of Standards, 1963. 191 pp.

PERIODICALS

412 *Communications of the ACM*. New York: Association for Computing Machinery, 1958 —. Monthly. [Contains section on Computational Linguistics.]

413 *Computing Reviews*. New York: Association for Computing Machinery, 1960 —. Bimonthly.

414 *The Finite String*. Newsletter of the Association for Machine Translation and Computational Linguistics. Cleveland, Ohio, 1964 —. 10 nos. a yr.

415 *Information and Control*. New York: Academic Press, 1957 —. 4 nos. a yr.

416 *Keiryô Kokugogaku*. Tokyo: Mathematical Linguistic Society of Japan, 1957 —. Quarterly.

417 *Lenguaje y Ciencias*. Trujillo, Peru: Cátedra de Idiomas Modernos, Universidad Nacional de Trujillo, 1961 —. 3 nos. a yr.

418 *MT: Mechanical Translation*. Devoted to the translation of languages with the aid of machines. Cambridge, Mass.: Massachusetts Institute of Technology, 1954 —. Irregular.

419 *The Prague Bulletin of Mathematical Linguistics*. Prague: Karlova Univ., 1964 —. Semiannual.

420 *Statistical Methods in Linguistics*. Stockholm: Språkförlaget Skriptor, 1961 —. Semiannual. [Text in English, German, and French.]

421 *La Traduction Automatique*. Bulletin trimestriel de l'Association pour l'étude et le Développement de la Traduction automatique et de la Linguistique appliquée. The Hague: Mouton, 1960 —. 4 nos. a yr. [Text in English and French. Contains large "bibliography" and "abstract" sections.]

MONOGRAPHS

422 *Center for Information Sciences Reports*. Bethlehem, Pa.: Lehigh Univ., 1963 —.

423 *Foreign Developments in Machine Translation and Information Processing*. Washington, D.C.: Joint Publications Research Service, Office of Technical Services, U.S. Department of Commerce, 1957 —.

424 *Georgetown University Occasional Papers on Machine Translation*. Washington, D.C.: Institute of Languages and Linguistics, Machine Translation Research Center, 1959 —.

425 *Linguistic and Engineering Studies in Automatic Language Translation*. Seattle, Wash.; Univ. of Washington, 1956 —.

426 *Linguistic Research Center Working Papers*. Austin, Tex.: Univ. of Texas, 1958 —.

427   *Mathematical Linguistics and Automatic Translation.* Cambridge, Mass. Computational Laboratory, Harvard Univ., 1959 —.

428   *Mechanolinguistic Project Papers.* Berkeley, Calif.: Univ. of California, 1962 —.

429   *Project on Linguistic Ana'ysis Reports.* Columbus, Ohio: Ohio State Univ., 1962 —.

430   *Transformations and Discourse Analysis Papers.* Philadelphia: Univ. of Pennsylvania, 1958 —.

HISTORIES AND SURVEYS

431   Abernathy, Robert. "Soviet mathematical linguistics." *Current Trends* [079], 113–32.

432   Harper, Kenneth E. "Machine translation." *Current Trends* [079], 133–42.

433   Hymes, Dell H. "Lexicostatistics so far." *Current Anthropology* 1.3–44 (1960).

434   Plath, Warren. "Mathematical linguistics." *Trends I* [074], 22–57.

THEORY AND METHOD

435   Andrejev, N. D., ed. *Materialy po matematičeskoj lingvistike i mašinnomu perevodu* [Materials or mathematical linguistics and machine translation]. Leningrad: Leningradskogo Univ., 1963. 195 pp.

436   Apostel, Léo, Benoît Mandelbrot and Albert Morf. *Logique, langage et théorie de l'information.* Paris: Presses Univ. de France, 1957. 207 pp.

437   Axmanova, O. S., I. A. Mel'čuk, R. M. Frumkina and E. V. Padučeva. *O točnyx metodax issleaovanija jazyka.* Moscow: Izd. Moskovskogo. Univ., 1961. 162 pp. Trans. David G. Hays and Dolores V. Mohr, *Exact methods in linguistic research.* Berkeley, Calif.: Univ. of California Press, 1963.

438   Belevitch, V. *Langage des machines et langage humain.* Brussels: Office de Publicité, 1956. 121 pp.

439   Ceccato, S., ed. *Linguistic analysis and programming for mechanical translation.* New York: Gordon & Breach, 1962. 242 pp.

440   Cooper, William S. *Set theory and syntactic description.* (Janua Linguarum, Series Minor, 34.) The Hague: Mouton, 1964. 52 pp.

441   Delavenay, E. *La machine à traduire.* Paris: Presses Univ. de France, 1959. 126 pp. Trans. *An introduction to machine translation.* New York: Praeger, 1960.

442   Edmundson, H. P., ed. *Proceedings of the national symposium on machine translation.* Englewood Cliffs, N.J.: Prentice-Hall, 1961. 525 pp.

443 Garvin, Paul L., ed. *Nautral language and the computer*. New York: McGraw-Hill, 1963. 398 pp.

444 Guiraud, Pierre. *Problèmes et méthodes de la statistique linguistique*. Paris: Presses Univ. de France, 1960. 145 pp.

445 Herdan, Gustav. *The calculus of linguistic observations*. (Janua Linguarum, Series Maior, 9.) The Hague: Mouton, 1962. 271 pp.

446 ———. *Language as choice and chance*. Groningen: Noordhoff, 1956. 356 pp.

447 ———. *Type-token mathematics: A textbook of mathematical linguistics*. (Janua Linguarum, Series Maior, 4.) The Hague: Mouton, 1960. 448 pp.

448 Jakobson, Roman, ed. *Structure of language and its mathematical aspects*. Providence, R.I.: American Mathematical Society, 1961. 279 pp.

449 *Lexico-statistic issue*. International Journal of American Linguistics 21:2.91–177 (1955).

450 Locke, William N. and A. Donald Booth, eds. *Machine translation of languages*. Cambridge, Mass.: M.I.T. Press, 1955. 243 pp.

451 Mounin, Georges. *La machine à traduire: Histoire des problèmes linguistiques*. (Janua Linguarum, Series Minor, 32.) The Hague: Mouton, 1964. 209 pp.

452 Oettinger, Anthony G. *Automatic language translation: Lexical and technical aspects, with particular reference to Russian*. (Harvard Monographs in Applied Science, 8.) Cambridge, Mass.: Harvard Univ. Press, 1960. 380 pp.

453 Panov, G. J. *Avtomatičeskii perevod* [Automatic translation]. 2nd ed. Moscow: Izd. Akad. Nauk SSSR, 1958. 48 pp.

454 *Proceedings of the international conference on machine translation of languages and applied language analysis*. 2 vols. London: Her Majesty's Stationery Office, 1962.

455 Revzin, I. I. *Modeli jazyka*. Moscow: Izd. Akad. Nauk SSSR, 1962. 191 pp. Trans. *Language models*, Washington, D.C.: JPRS, Office of Technical Services, Dept. of Commerce, 1963.

456 Shannon, Claude E. and Warren Weaver. *The mathematical theory of communication*. Urbana, Ill.: Univ. of Illinois Press, 1949. 117 pp. (Paperback edition: Illini IB–13.)

Part 3: Applied Linguistics

3.1. General Works

PERIODICALS

457 *Cahiers de Linguistique Théoretique et Appliquée.* See [019].

458 *IRAL: International Review of Applied Linguistics in Language Teaching.* Heidelberg: J. Groos, 1963 —. Quarterly. [Text in several languages.]

459 *The Linguistic Reporter.* Newsletter of the Center for Applied Linguistics. Washington, D.C., 1959 —. 6 nos. a yr. plus supplements.

460 *Language Learning: A Journal of Applied Linguistics.* Ann Arbor, Mich.: Research Club in Language Learning, 1948 —. Quarterly.

461 *Die Neuren Sprachen.* Zeitschrift für Forschung und Unterricht auf dem Fachgebiet der modernen Fremdsprachen. Frankfurt am Main: Moritz Diesterweg, 1952 —. Monthly.

462 *RLA: Revista de Lingüística Aplicada.* Publicación del Círculo Lingüístico de la Universidad de Concepción. Concepción, Chile, 1963 —. Irregular.

HISTORIES AND SURVEYS

463 van Teslaar, A. P. "Les domaines de la linguistique appliquée." *IRAL* 1.50–77, 223–78 (1963). [Parts 1 and 2 of a bibliographical survey. Part 3 to appear.]

THEORY AND METHOD

464 Allen, Harold B., ed. *Readings in applied English linguistics.* 2nd ed. Appleton-Century-Crofts, 1963. 535 pp.

3.2. Language Teaching

BIBLIOGRAPHY

465 "Annotated bibliography of modern language methodology for 19 —." *Modern Language Journal* [474], 1916 —. Annual.

466 Coleman, Algernon. *An analytical bibliography of modern language teaching.* 3 vols. Chicago: Univ. of Chicago Press, 1933–49. Vol. 1, 1927–1932; Vol. 2, 1932–1937; Vol. 3, 1937–1942. [Vol. 3 has imprint: New York: King's Crown Press.]

34 [467–481]

467 Ferguson, Charles A. and William A. Stewart, eds. *Linguistic reading lists for teachers of modern languages.* Washington, D.C.: Center for Applied Linguistics, 1963. 114 pp.

468 Nostrand, Howard Lee, and others. *Research on language teaching: An annotated international bibliography for 1945–61.* Seattle, Wash.: Univ. of Washington Press, 1962. 280 pp.

469 Tharp, James B., ed. *Annotated bibliographies of modern-language methodology for the years 1946, 1947, and 1948.* Columbus, Ohio: Ohio State Univ., 1952. 74 pp.

470 UNESCO. *A bibliography on the teaching of modern languages.* (UNESCO Educational Studies and Documents, 13.) Paris: UNESCO, 1955. 107 pp.

PERIODICALS

471 *Canadian Modern Language Review.* Toronto: Ontario Modern Language Teachers' Assoc., 1944 —. Quarterly.

472 *Inostrannye Jazyki v Škole.* Moscow: Ministerstvo Prosveščenija, 1937 —. 6 nos. a yr.

473 *Les Langues Modernes.* Paris: Association des Professeurs de Langues Vivantes de L'enseignement Public, 1903 —. 6 nos a yr.

474 *Modern Language Journal.* Menasha, Wisc.: National Federation of Modern Language Teachers' Associations, 1916 —. 8 nos. a yr.

475 *Modern Languages.* Journal of the Modern Language Association. London, 1905 —. Quarterly.

476 *Moderna Språk.* Saltsjö-Duvnäs, Sweden: Modern Language Teachers' Association of Sweden, 1907 —. 4 nos. a yr.

HISTORIES AND SURVEYS

477 Moulton, William G. "Linguistics and language teaching in the United States 1940–1960." *Trends I* [074], 82–109. (Offprint: U.S. Government Printing Office, Washington, D.C.)

478 Ornstein, Jacob. "Foreign language teaching." *Current Trends* [079], 143–91.

THEORY AND METHOD

479 Bloomfield, Leonard. *Outline guide for the practical study of foreign languages.* Baltimore: Linguistic Society of America, 1942. 16 pp.

480 Brooks, Nelson. *Language and language learning: Theory and practice.* 2nd ed. New York: Harcourt, Brace & World, 1964. 300 pp.

481 Dunkel, Harold B. *Second-language learning.* Boston: Ginn, 1948. 218 pp.

482 Fries, Charles C. *Teaching and learning English as a foreign language*. Ann Arbor, Mich.: Univ. of Michigan Press, 1945. 153 pp.

483 Halliday, M. A. K., Angus McIntosh and Peter Strevens. *The linguistic sciences and language teaching*. London: Longmans, 1964. 344 pp.

484 Jespersen, Otto. *How to teach a foreign language*. New York: Macmillan, 1904. 194 pp.

485 Lado, Robert. *Language teaching: A scientific approach*. New York: McGraw-Hill, 1963. 239 pp.

486 ———. *Linguistics across cultures: Applied linguistics for language teachers*. Ann Arbor, Mich.: Univ of Michigan Press, 1957. 141 pp.

487 Newmark, Maxim, ed. *Twentieth century modern language teaching*. New York: Philosophical Library, 1948. 723 pp.

488 Nida, Eugene A. *Learning a foreign language*. Rev. ed. New York: Friendship Press, 1957. 212 pp.

489 Palmer, H. E. *The scientific study and teaching of languages*. Yonkers-on-Hudson: World Book, 1917. 328 pp.

490 Pittman, Dean. *Practical linguistics*. Cleveland, Ohio: Mid-Missions, 1948. 229 pp.

491 Rivers, Wilga A. *The psychologist and the foreign-language teacher*. Chicago: Univ. of Chicago Press, 1964. 212 pp.

492 Sweet, Henry. *The practical study of languages: A guide for teachers and learners*. New York: Holt, 1900. 280 pp.

3.3. Translation

BIBLIOGRAPHY

493 Morgan, Bayard Quincy. "A critical bibliography of works on translation." *On Translation* [500], 269–93.

PERIODICALS

494 *Babel: Revue Internationale de la Traduction*. Paris: Fédération Internationale de Traducteurs, 1955 —. Quarterly. [Text in several languages.]

495 *The Bible Translator*. Amsterdam: United Bibles Societies, 1950 —. Quarterly.

496 *The Incorporated Linguist*. London: The Institute of Linguists, 1962 —. Quarterly. [Formerly *Linguists' Review*, 1924–1962.]

497 *MT: Mechanical Translation*. See [418].

498 *La Traduction Automatique*. See [421].

THEORY AND METHOD

499   Booth, A. Donald, and others. *Aspects of translation*. London: Secker & Warburg, 1958. 145 pp.

500   Brower, Reuben A., ed. *On translation*. Cambridge, Mass.: Harvard Univ. Press, 1959. 298 pp.

501   Fedorov, A. V. *Vvedenie v teoriju perevoda* [An introduction to the theory of translation]. 2nd ed. Moscow: Izd. Lit. na Inostr. Jazykax, 1958. 336 pp.

502   Nida, Eugene A. *Bible translating*. New York: American Bible Society, 1947. 362 pp.

503   ———. *Toward a science of translating, with special reference to principles and procedures involved in Bible translating*. Leiden: Brill, 1964. 331 pp.

504   *Translation issue*. International Journal of American Linguistics 20:4.259–340 (1954).

3.4. Stylistics

505   Epstein, Edmund L. and Terence Hawkes. *Linguistics and English prosody* (with an introduction by Henry Lee Smith, Jr.). (Studies in Linguistics: Occasional Papers, 7.) Buffalo, N.Y.: Univ. of Buffalo, 1959. 50 pp.

506   Garvin, Paul L., ed. and trans. *A Prague School reader on esthetics, literary structure and style*. Washington, D.C.: Georgetown Univ. Press, 1964. 163 pp.

507   Guiraud, Pierre. *La stylistique*. Paris: Presses Univ. de France, 1954. 119 pp.

508   Levin, S. R. *Linguistic structures in poetry*. (Janua Linguarum, Series Minor, 19.) The Hague: Mouton, 1962. 64 pp.

509   *Poetics*. Papers of the International Conference of Work-in-Progress Devoted to the Problems of Poetics, Warsaw, 1960. The Hague: Mouton, 1960. 895 pp.

510   Sebeok, Thomas A., ed. *Style in language*. Cambridge, Mass.: M.I.T. Press, 1960. 470 pp.

511   Spencer, John, M. Gregory and N. Enkvist. *Linguistics and style*. London: Oxford Univ. Press, 1965.

512   Spitzer, Leo. *Linguistics and literary history: Essays in stylistics*. New York: Russel & Russel, 1962 [c. 1948]. 236 pp.

513   Ullmann, Stephen. *Language and Style: Collected Papers*. Oxford: Blackwell, 1964. 270 pp.

514 *Abstracts of English studies.* Boulder, Colo.: National Council of Teachers of English, 1958 —. Monthly.

515 *African abstracts.* A quarterly review of ethnological, social and linguistic studies appearing in current periodicals. London: International African Institute, 1950 —. Quarterly.

516 *Bulletin de la Société de Linguistique de Paris.* See [018].
   Each issue contains a large review section, which can serve as an abstracting service.

517 *Bulletin signalétique.* Sect on 21: *Sociologie et Sciences du langage.* Paris: Centre National de la Recherche Scientifique, 1961 —. Quarterly. [Formerly included in section 3, *Philosophie et Sciences humaines,* 1956–1960, and *Bulletin analytique: Philosophie,* 1947–1955.]

518 *Current research and development in scientific documentation.* Washington, D.C.: National Science Foundation, 1957 —. 2 nos. a yr.

519 *Dissertation abstracts.* A guide to dissertations and monographs available in microfilm. Ann Arbor, Mich.: University Microfilms, 1952 —. Monthly. [Formerly *Microfilm abstracts,* 1938–51.]

520 *Doctoral dissertations.* New York: Wilson, 1934–55. Annual. [Beginning in 1956, material included in *Dissertation abstracts.*]

521 *English-Teaching abstracts.* London: English-Teaching Information Centre, The British Council, 1961 —. Quarterly.

522 *International Journal of American Linguistics.* See [027].
   Beginning 1961, each issue contains abstract section.

523 *Masters abstracts.* Abstracts of selected masters theses on microfilm. Ann Arbor, Mich.: University Microfilms, 1962 —. Irregular.

524 *Microfilm abstracts.* Ann Arbor, Mich.: University Microfilms, 1938–51. [Continued as *Dissertation abstracts.*]

525 *MLabstracts.* Fullerton Calif.: Orange County State College, 1961 —. 3 nos. a yr.

526 *La Traduction Automatique.* See [421].
   Each issue contains abstract section.

527 *Voprosy Jazykoznanija* See [046].
   Each issue contains abstract section.

Part 5: Classification Systems

528   Dewey, Melvil. *Dewey decimal classification and relative index.* 16th ed. 2 vols. Essex County, N.Y.: Forest Press, 1958.

529   Trager, George L. "A bibliographical classification system for linguistics." *Studies in Linguistics* 3.54–108 (1945), 4.1–50 (1946). "Additions and corrections . . ." 6.17–19 (1948); "Revisions . . . 1." 6.98–9 (1948); "Revisions . . . 2." 9.91–93 (1951).

530   U.S. Library of Congress. *Outline of Library of Congress classification.* Washington, D.C., 1942 (reprinted 1955), and further breakdowns issued in separate volumes. Especially note: Library of Congress Classification Schedule Class P, Philology and Literature, Subclass P–PA, *Philology, linguistics, classical philology, classical literature,* 1928 (reprinted 1955). As above, Subclass PB–PH, *Modern European languages,* 1933 (reprinted 1957). As above, Subclass PJ–PM, *Languages and literatures of Asia, Africa, Oceania, America, mixed languages, artificial languages,* 1935 (reprinted 1956). As above, Subclass P–PM, supplement, *Index to languages and dialects,* 1957.

531   *Universal decimal classification.* Abridged English ed. 3rd rev. ed. London: British Standards Institution, 1961.

532   *Guide to the universal decimal classification.* London: British Standards Institution, 1963.

533   Bower, William W. *International manual of linguists and translators.* New York: Scarecrow Press, 1959. 451 pp.

534   *Directory of American scholars.* 4th ed. 4 vols. New York: Bowker, 1963–64.
Vol. III, *Foreign languages (modern and classical), linguistics and philology,* contains approximately 5100 biographies.

535   *National register of scientific and technical personnel in the field of linguistics and allied specialties.*
Conducted since March 1964 by the Center for Applied Linguistics and the National Science Foundation in cooperation with the Linguistic Society of America. Supplemented and revised biennially. Includes only American citizens and foreign nationals resident in the U.S. Information used by NSF for statistical reports on manpower situation in the sciences.

536   *Roster of linguists.* A register of specialists in linguistics and related fields.
Project administered by the Center for Applied Linguistics since December 1960. Includes both American citizens and foreign nationals. Information used primarily by CAL for preparation of lists of specialists in specific fields.

537   UNESCO. *Social scientists specializing in African studies.* Paris & The Hague: Mouton, 1963. 375 pp.
An international directory. Contains 2,072 brief biographies, 113 of which come under the subject heading "Linguistics, including terminology."

Author Index

Abernathy, R. 431
Aguirre, M. 235
Albright, R. W. 141
Allen, H. B. 464
Allen, W. S. 142
American Council of Learned Societies 352
Andrejev, N. D. 126, 435
Andrews, S., Jr. 066
Apostel, L. 436
Arens, H. 067
Austerlitz, R. 084
Axmanova, O. S. 173, 209, 379, 437

Bach, A. 221
Bach, E. 174
Baldinger, K. 189
Bally, C. 353
Balz, C. F. 403
Bartoli, M. 222
Bastian, J. R. 390
Bateson, M. C. 327
Battisti, C. 068
Bazell, C. E. 085
Belevitch, V. 438
Bloch, B. 086, 231
Bloch, J. 231
Bloomfield, L. 087, 479
Booth, A. D. 450, 499
Bower, W. W. 533
Boyd, J. C. 171
Bram, J. 354
Bréal, M. 190
Brooks, N. 480
Brower, R. A. 500
Brown, R. 321
Bühler, K. 380
Bursill-Hall, G. L. 172

Cantineau, J. 166
Carroll, J. B. 323, 324, 381
Casares, J. 210
Cassidy, F. G. 223
Ceccato, S. 439
Chapman, R. W. 211
Cherry, C. 322
Chomsky, N. 175, 176
Cofer, C. N. 382, 383
Cohen, M. 063, 088, 224, 236, 237, 355, 395
Coleman, A. 466

Collison, R. L. 202
Comité International Permanent des Linguistes 004
Cooper, W. S. 440
Coseriu, E. 225
Cust, Mrs. H. 190

Dauzat, A. 226
Degering, H. 238
Delavenay, E. 404, 441
Delavenay, K. 404
Dewey, M. 528
Diringer, D. 239, 240
Diver, W. 084
Dubsky, J. 128
Duckett, J. 347
Duncan, H. D. 356
Dunkel, H. B. 481

Eaton, H. S. 191
Edmont, E. 227
Edmundson, H. P. 442
Elson, B. 177
English Association 007
Enkvist, N. 511
Epstein, E. L. 505

Fedorov, A. V. 501
Felice, E. de 122
Ferguson, C. A. 357, 467
Février, J. G. 241
Firth, J. R. 089
Fries, C. C. 070, 482
Frumkina, R. M. 437

Gabain, M. 388
Gage, W. W. 006
Garvin, P. L. 443, 506
Gaynor, F. 127
Gelb, I. J. 242
Giljarevskij, R. S. 243
Gilliéron, J. 227, 228
Gipper, H. 405
Gleason, H. A., Jr. 112
Godel, R. 071
Goodell, R. J. 329
Grammont, M. 143
Gray, L. H. 090
Green, H. C. 161
Greenberg, J. H. 091, 092
Grivnin, V. S. 243

Grégoire, A.   396
Gregory, M.   511
Guiraud, P.   192, 406, 444, 507
Gumperz, J. J.   357
Guxman, M. M.   358
Gvozdev, A. N.   397

Hall, R. A., Jr.   072, 093
Halle, M.   144
Halliday, M. A. K.   483
Hallig, R.   212
Hallowell, A. I.   328
Hammer, J. H.   006
Hamp, E. P.   073, 123
Hanfmann, E.   393
Hansen, M. L.   231
Harper, K. E.   432
Harris, Z.   113, 178
Hattori, S.   061
Haugen, E.   346
Hawkes, T.   505
Hayes, A. S.   327
Hays, D. G.   407, 408, 437
Heffner, R.-M. S.   145
Henle, P.   325
Herdan, G.   445, 446, 447
Higounet, C.   244
Hill, A. A.   114
Hjelmslev, L.   094, 095, 179
Hockett, C. F.   096, 146
Hoenigswald, H. M.   117
Hoijer, H.   340, 343
Householder, F. W.   213
Hymes, D. H.   330, 341, 344, 433

Ichikawa, S.   061
International Phonetic Association   147
Istrin, V. A.   245

Jaberg, K.   229, 230
Jakobson, R.   148, 149, 345, 398, 448
Jensen, H.   246
Jespersen, O.   097, 180, 359, 484
Jones, D.   150
Jones, L. G.   144
Joos, M.   115, 151, 181, 384
Jud, J.   230
Juilland, A. G.   182

Kahane, H.   399
Kahane, R.   399
Kaiser, L.   152
Katz, J. J.   098
King, H. V.   171
Knobloch, J.   124
Kopp, G. A.   161
Kôzu, H.   061
Krejči, K.   360

Kronasser, H.   193
Kurath, H.   231

Ladefoged, P.   153
Lado, R.   485, 486
Lamb, S. M.   183
Lehmann, W. P.   118
Leopold, W. F.   394, 400
Levi-Strauss, C.   345
Levin, S. R.   508
Lewis, K.   347
Lewis, M. M.   361, 401
Locke, W. N.   450
Longacre, R. E.   184

McIntosh, A.   232, 483
Malmberg, B.   099
Mandelbrot, B.   436
Mandlebaum, D. G.   326
Marouzeau, J.   125, 126
Martinet, A.   084, 100, 101, 154, 155, 156
Matoré, G.   214
Meillet, A.   063, 102, 119
Mel'čuk, I. A.   437
Mikaèljar, G. B.   173
Milewski, T.   064
Miller, G. A.   385
Modern Humanities Research Association   008
Mohr, D. V.   437
Mohrmann, C.   074, 075
Mol, H.   157
Morf, A.   436
Morgan, B. Q.   493
Moulton, W. G.   477
Mounin, G.   451
Muller, S. H.   065
Musgrave, B. S.   382, 383

Newman, S. S.   328
Newmark, M.   487
Nida, E. A.   185, 186, 488, 502, 503
Norman, F.   075
North, E. M.   247
Nostrand, H. L.   468

Oettinger, A. G.   452
Olmsted, D. L.   342
Ornstein, J.   478
Osgood, C. E.   386, 387

Padučeva, E. V.   437
Palmer, H. E.   248, 489
Panov, G. J.   453
Paul, H.   120
Pedersen, H.   076
Pei, M.   127

41

Piaget, J. 388
Pickett, V. B. 177
Pietrzyk, A. 347
Pike, K. L. 103, 158, 159, 160
Pittman, D. 490
Plath, W. 434
Pop, S. 215, 233
Postal, P. M. 098, 187
Potter, R. K. 161
Pronko, N. H. 378
Pulgram, E. 162

Radin, P. 110
Ray, P. S. 364
Revzin, I. I. 455
Rice, F. A. 365
Rivers, W. A. 491
Robins, R. H. 077, 078, 104
Robinson, R. 194
Roques, M. 228

Sapir, E. 105, 326
Saporta, S. 213, 390, 399
Sattler, P. 234
Šaumjan, S. K. 163
Saussure, F. de 106
Savitz, L. 348
Schwarz, H. 405
Sebeok, T. A. 079, 130, 327, 345, 386, 510
Segerstedt, T. T. 366
Shannon, C. E. 456
Siegel, B. J. 331
Skinner, B. F. 391
Smalley, W. A. 164, 249
Smith, H. L., Jr. 116, 505
Sommerfelt, A. 074, 075, 080, 107, 367
Spencer, J. 511
Spier, L. 328
Spitzer, L. 512
Sprang-Hanssen, H. 081
Stanwood, R. H. 403
Stern, G. 195
Stetson, R. H. 165
Stewart, W. A. 467

Strevens, P. 483
Suci, G. J. 387
Sweet, H. 492

Tannenbaum, P. H. 387
Tesnière, L. 188
Tharp, J. B. 469
Titone, R. 392
Trager, G. L. 086, 108, 116, 529
Trier, J. 196
Trubetskoy, N. S. 166
Twaddell, W. F. 167

Uldall, H. J. 095
Ullmann, S. 197, 198, 513
UNESCO 203, 470, 537
U.S. Library of Congress 010, 011, 204, 530

Vachek, J. 109, 128
Vakar, G. 393
van Teslaar, A. P. 463
Vendryès, J. 110
Vildomec, V. 362
Voegelin, C. F. 345
von Essen, O. 168
von Selle, G. 234
von Wartburg, W. 121, 212
Vygotsky, L. S. 393

Walkowicz, J. L. 411
Ward, I. C. 169
Waterman, J. T. 082
Weaver, W. 456
Weinreich, U. 084, 101, 208, 369
Weir, R. H. 402
Westermann, D. 169
Whatmough, J. 066, 074, 111, 190
Whitfield, F. J. 094
Whorf, B. L. 323
Wise, C. M. 170

Zaunmüller, W. 205
Ziff, P. 199
Zvegincev, V. A. 083, 200

COMPOSED AND PRINTED BY THE AMERICAN INTERNATIONAL PRINTING COMPANY, SILVER SPRING, MARYLAND